privacy in the
ONLINE WORLD

Online Privacy and Hacking

John Allen

ReferencePoint Press®

San Diego, CA

About the Author

John Allen is a writer who lives in Oklahoma City.

For more information, contact:
ReferencePoint Press, Inc.
PO Box 27779
San Diego, CA 92198
www. ReferencePointPress.com

Picture Credits
Maury Aaseng: 6; AP Images: 37; © Jim Bennett/Corbis: 10; © Chip East/Reuters/Corbis: 26; © Furgolle/BSIP/Corbis: 45; © Rick Gomez/Corbis: 16; © Raheb Homavandi/Reuters/Corbis: 28; © James Leynse/Corbis: 38; © Sage Ross/dpa/Corbis: 61; © Mike Segar/Reuters/Corbis: 22; © Ted Soqui/Corbis: 58; Thinkstock Images: 34; © Alex Milan Tracey/Demotix/Corbis: 55; © Leigh Vogel/Corbis: 51

LIBRARY OF CONGRESS CATALOGING-IN-PUBLICATION DATA

Allen, John.
Online privacy and hacking / by John Allen.
pages cm. — (Privacy in the online world)
Audience: Grade 9 to 12.
Includes bibliographical references and index.
ISBN-13: 978-1-60152-728-8 (hardback)
ISBN-10: 1-60152-728-4 (hardback)
1. Internet and children—Juvenile literature. 2. Online identity theft—Juvenile literature.
3. Internet—Security measures—Juvenile literature. I. Title.
HQ784.I58.A45 2014
302.3—dc23

2014020442

Contents

Introduction

A Holiday Hacking Attack

On December 19, 2013, Minneapolis-based department store chain Target revealed that payment card data for at least 40 million of its customers had been illegally accessed by computer hackers. Upscale retailer Neiman Marcus admitted its own breach, with about 1.1 million payment cards hacked. These announcements confirmed a series of stories by a cybersecurity blogger and set in motion a nightmare scenario for the retailers. For several days during the holiday shopping season the news kept going from bad to worse. Target faced a growing number of lawsuits from angry customers and banks. Scam artists posing as concerned Target employees or bank representatives began contacting Target shoppers, and the company had to warn its customers not to give out personal information over the phone. Target soon discovered that personal identification numbers (PINs) associated with the hacked credit cards were also exposed. As the story developed, Target's liabilities were estimated at more than $3.5 billion. The number of Target customers affected grew to 110 million. In March 2014 reports linked the cyberattack to a ring of hackers in the Black Sea port of Odessa in Ukraine.

Apparently Target could have prevented the theft but failed to do so. In interviews with Target cybersecurity employees *Bloomberg Businessweek* discovered that Target had protective software in place and a team in Bangalore, India, monitoring its computer systems for just such a breach. According to *Bloomberg Businessweek*'s reporters, "The story [Target's employees] tell is of an alert system, installed to protect the bond between retailer and customer, that worked beautifully. But then, Target stood by as 40 million credit card numbers—and 70 million addresses, phone numbers, and other pieces of personal information—gushed out of its mainframes."[1]

Apparently the company's people in Bangalore saw the software alerts about a possible breach and informed the security team in Minneapolis in plenty of time to avert the attack. However, the Minneapolis team failed to act. What is more, outside experts said the thieves' methods were nothing special. "The malware utilized is absolutely unsophisticated and uninteresting,"[2] said Jim Walter, director of threat intelligence operations at security technology company McAfee. As is often the case, the perpetrators had benefited from the weakest link in the system: the human element.

Lawbreaking Hackers

> "Target stood by as 40 million credit card numbers—and 70 million addresses, phone numbers, and other pieces of personal information—gushed out of its mainframes."[1]
>
> —*Michael Riley, Ben Elgin, Dune Lawrence, and Carol Matlack in* Bloomberg Businessweek.

Target's and Neiman Marcus's customers, not to mention the companies themselves, were only the latest victims of an activity called hacking. Those who use their computer skills to gain unauthorized access to information online or on a connected system are known as hackers. Actually the great majority of hackers are not lawbreakers at all. They generally access a system in order to do something that is different from or beyond the creator's original purpose. However, in the media the term *hacking* has become almost synonymous with cybercrime. (Law-abiding hackers sometimes use the term "black hat hackers" to refer to the illicit ones.)

Just as the Internet has enabled users to do everything from shopping to playing games online, it has also led to virtual crimes such as theft and sabotage. The hackers who attacked Target sought customers' PINs and payment card numbers, along with other personal information, in order to sell them to other illegal users or use them themselves to make illegal purchases. Movies and television shows often depict hackers as young, computer-savvy "nerds" who enjoy testing their skills against the safety measures employed by the federal government or large corporations to protect their data systems. Criminal hackers are not in it for the sport, however. They doggedly troll the Internet in search of vulnerable systems. The Target case shows just how much damage can be done by even relatively unsophisticated cyberthieves.

Troubling New Threats to Privacy

With the rise of the Internet and today's interconnected, computerized world have come troubling new threats to privacy and personal information. Stories like the Target hacking increase people's anxiety about sharing information online. Yet the whole idea of privacy has changed radically in only a generation. Today many people not only make purchases online using credit card numbers but also share intimate personal details via social media such as Facebook, LinkedIn, and Twitter. Search engines and websites gather and maintain mountains of information about users. When a person does online research for a planned vacation, ads from airlines and hotels follow from page to page. A sudden interest in scrapbooks, rock climbing, or gardening will summon a flurry of helpful ads and websites. Those who find such tracking obtrusive and worrisome would probably be shocked at all the ways a dedicated hacker can affect a person's life in today's cyberlinked world. From accessing voice mail to disabling home security systems to stealing a person's online identity, malicious hackers can cause all sorts of mischief. Hackers' motivations are also not limited to financial gain. Some use hacking to pursue political goals, while others seek revenge against individuals or groups or simply want to create chaos.

> "We entrust some incredibly sensitive information to online dating sites. People don't realize how much information they're exposing even by doing something as slight as uploading a photograph."[3]
>
> *—Rainey Reitman, Electronic Frontier Foundation.*

Society continues to wrestle with issues of privacy even as new technologies appear every month. People must weigh the ease and convenience of doing business or sharing information online with the possibility of invasion of privacy by dedicated hackers. The most mundane activities can present problems. For example, questions have recently been raised about the rapidly growing online dating industry. "We entrust some incredibly sensitive information to online dating sites," says Rainey Reitman of the San Francisco–based Electronic Frontier Foundation, a nonprofit group that advocates for user privacy amid technology development. "People don't realize how much information they're exposing even by doing something as slight as uploading a photograph."[3] Similar concerns exist about using a debit card to get cash at an automatic teller machine (ATM) or even presenting a driver's license as photo ID, with all the additional personal information many licenses contain. Horror stories about people who have had their identities stolen by hackers are leading many people to be increasingly wary. Ultimately each individual must decide how much information to share online and how trustworthy are the depths of cyberspace.

Chapter 1

A Look at Privacy Concerns

Before the advent of personal computers and the Internet, maintaining privacy and securing personal information meant keeping important documents and financial material locked away in a safety deposit box or home safe, or at least hidden away from possible theft. Today, however, information about every aspect of a person's life is often electronically available—and vulnerable to computer hackers. Recent polls reveal the level of anxiety created by this state of affairs. A November 2013 survey found that Internet users are much more worried about theft of their personal and financial information than about companies tracking them online in order to target them for advertising. According to Ed Black, president and chief executive of the Computer and Communications Industry Association, which sponsored the poll, "By wide margins this survey clearly shows that identity theft has touched the majority of consumers in some way, and that hacking is more worrisome to consumers than tracking, and that voters want the government to more aggressively go after cyber criminals."[4] A July 2013 study by the Pew Internet & American Life Project found that a large majority of Internet users take steps to remove or mask their digital footprints in order to foil hackers. Recent headlines have apparently only increased the uneasiness. In April 2014 a Harris poll discovered that people were doing less shopping, banking, and personal communication online due to revelations about government surveillance of the Internet. In 2013 an American computer contractor named Edward Snowden caused a firestorm when he leaked classified documents that showed how the US National Security Agency collects and stores information on citizens—a process called data mining. Results of the Harris poll surprised many experts who had never before seen a decline in Internet usage.

In general, there is a divide between younger individuals who have grown up with the Internet and are comfortable sharing information online and older people who are more leery about potential problems. Certainly the concept of privacy has undergone a huge transformation in the computer age. Some observers compare today's changing ideas about privacy to past societal changes that brought about new attitudes on racial equality and sexual mores. Privacy issues will doubtless continue to spark a great deal of controversy in coming years.

Privacy and the Mail

Throughout history an important measure of privacy has been the ability to communicate in a confidential manner. Long ago, messages were delivered on scrolls tied with string, with no way to tell if someone other than the intended recipient had read them. In the seventeenth century a method of securing letters with sealing wax was developed in western Europe. An intact circular red seal showed that a message had not been tampered with—although seals might also be cracked or broken with rough handling. In 1710 England's Parliament placed an emphasis on privacy by passing the Post Office Act, which specified that mail must not be opened, detained, or delayed and that violators would be subjected to stiff fines. The first American Postal Service began in 1775, with Congress voting in 1782 to enforce confidentiality for the nation's mail. Benjamin Franklin, the United States' first postmaster, forbade his postal employees from opening bags of mail, yet he also assumed that his own letters were probably being opened and read. In the mid-1800s mass-produced envelopes replaced sealing wax and offered improved privacy for letters. Nevertheless, as demonstrated by spies or busybodies in a dozen old movies, even a sealed

> "This survey clearly shows that identity theft has touched the majority of consumers in some way, and that hacking is more worrisome to consumers than tracking, and that voters want the government to more aggressively go after cyber criminals."[4]
>
> *—Ed Black, president and chief executive of the Computer and Communications Industry Association.*

Edward Snowden caused an uproar when he revealed that the US government was secretly collecting information on citizens.

envelope could be opened with steam from a teakettle or read through with the help of a candle or light bulb. To foil such attempts, military or government communications were sometimes sent by special courier or written in code. Over the years American citizens developed a strong trust in the confidentiality of postal communication. Today there are stiff penalties for interfering with mail in the United States, and people generally are confident that no one will intercept and read their letters.

Privacy and Electronic Communication

Electronic communication brought new concerns about privacy and interception of messages. In 1838 the American inventor Samuel Morse perfected a telegraph system that used pulses of electric current sent over a wire to produce written codes of dots and dashes on a strip of paper. The coded messages were then translated into words and delivered in the form of telegrams. By 1861 Western Union had built the first transcontinental telegraph line in North America, enabling rapid communication from coast to coast. Along with this new technology came new opportunities for invasion of privacy. Citizens who once suspected the government of tampering with the mail now viewed a private company like Western Union with suspicion, since it handled thousands of personal messages every day. To calm such fears, Western Union wrote regulations that prohibited its employees from divulging any information contained in the messages they sent, received, or delivered.

The telephone was invented in the 1870s, and subscriptions to phone service grew rapidly in the early years of the 1900s with the introduction of party lines—service lines shared by multiple people, from four to as many as thirty. Large party lines involved some sort of coded ringing for each customer, such as a long ring for one, two short rings for another, and so forth. When anyone who shared a party line received a call, any other person on the line could listen in simply by lifting the receiver. Telephone companies urged customers to respect each other's privacy, but eavesdropping was rampant. "One technical feature of party lines made it amusingly difficult to listen in undetected," writes privacy expert Frederick S. Lane. "As each receiver was lifted off the hook, the voltage on the line decreased, which lowered the volume of the call. If too many people decided to eavesdrop on a call, the speakers would end up having to shout at each other in order to be heard."[5]

Wiretapping

Widespread use of the telegraph and telephone also led to a new way of intercepting messages: wiretapping. A wiretap is a device that gains access to wired communication either at the switching station or somewhere along the wired lines. Soon after the invention of the telegraph and telephone, laws were passed making it illegal for an unauthorized person to listen in on a wired communication. It is even illegal for an individual to record his or her own phone conversation without the permission of the other person on the line. Laws covering government use of phone taps for law enforcement were slower to develop and generally allowed officials a large amount of latitude. The invention of the microphone in 1889 enabled eavesdroppers, including government agents, police officers, private detectives, and blackmailers, to listen in on conversations without being on the premises. This raised arguments about whether intercepting communications by electronic means actually constituted a crime.

In the twentieth century rapid changes in communication meant that old laws were often stretched to cover new technologies. Prosecutors argued that laws written to address wiretapping did not apply to wireless communication such as radio messages or even cordless telephones. Courts struggled to balance law enforcement needs with privacy protections. One landmark decision came in the 1928 case *Olmstead v. United States*, in which the Supreme Court ruled that wiretapping by federal agents did not constitute an illegal search under the Fourth Amendment. In a farsighted dissent that defended privacy rights, Justice Louis Brandeis wrote:

> Subtler and more far-reaching means of invading privacy have become available to the Government, by means far more effective than stretching upon the rack, to obtain disclosure in court of what is whispered in the closet. . . . The progress of science in furnishing the Government with means of espionage is not likely to stop with wire-tapping. Ways may some day be developed by which the Government, without removing papers from secret drawers, can reproduce them in court, and by which it will be enabled to expose to a jury the most intimate occurrences of the home.[6]

Despite Brandeis's warnings, J. Edgar Hoover, the director of the Federal Bureau of Investigation (FBI) and a strong supporter of surveillance technology, used the *Olmstead* decision as the basis for widespread wiretapping against not only suspected criminals and spies but also those with unpopular political views. In an attempt to rein in this practice, Congress created the Federal Communications Commission (FCC) in 1934. The FCC had jurisdiction over radio, telephone, and telegraph, and could impose penalties on anyone who

The Idea of Privacy as a Right

For centuries, concern about privacy for ordinary citizens accompanied the growth of democracy and political rights. In 1215 King John of England signed the Magna Carta (Great Charter), which asserted the rights of individuals against what had previously been the unlimited power of the state. As time passed, British common law began to recognize vague protections against physical interference with life and property. In the 1600s colonists in North America sought political and religious freedom from the British crown and had to make difficult trade-offs between privacy and community. The American Revolution and independence led to the US Constitution, with its Bill of Rights that protects free speech, free association, freedom from self-incrimination, and freedom from unreasonable search and seizure—all of which are important aspects of privacy.

Despite these provisions, the Constitution actually contains no explicit guarantee of a right to privacy. One of the first descriptions of such a right came in an 1890 article by Samuel Warren and Louis Brandeis titled "The Right to Privacy." "Recent inventions and business methods call attention to the next step which must be taken for the protection of the person," wrote Warren and Brandeis, "and for securing to the individual . . . the right 'to be let alone.'. . . Numerous mechanical devices threaten to make good the prediction that 'what is whispered in the closet shall be proclaimed from the house-tops.'" The authors could almost have been referring to today's controversies about social media and secret surveillance programs.

Quoted in Leah Burrows, "To Be Let Alone: Brandeis Foresaw Privacy Problems," *BrandeisNOW*, July 24, 2013. www.brandeis.edu.

intercepted and divulged wire messages without authorization. The commission had little effect on Hoover's activities, however, particularly during the anti-Communist scare of the late 1940s and 1950s. Many began to question where the line should be drawn between precautionary surveillance and invasion of privacy. In the late 1960s and early 1970s, abuses by the Nixon administration involving electronic surveillance of political enemies led to President Richard M. Nixon's impeachment and resignation. The episode left many citizens suspicious of government intrusion and looking for new ways to protect their privacy rights.

Social Security Cards and Credit Cards

As modern life gained speed and complexity in the twentieth century, a number of innovations combined to present new challenges to privacy rights. Welfare state programs in many countries assigned lifelong identification numbers to citizens. In the United States, each citizen is required to have a Social Security number (SSN) for use in tracking his or her earnings history and computing pension benefits under the Social Security Act of 1935. The nine-digit SSN has become the chief means of identifying individuals in the public and private sectors. In 1936 the government began giving each citizen a small card featuring her or his name and SSN, but with no accompanying photograph. A year later, when the first Social Security benefit checks were sent out, fraudsters began to steal the checks and cash them using fake cards for ID—an early instance of what is now called identity theft. Criminals also found it relatively easy to apply for new SSNs under fake names. Today so much personal information is keyed to an individual's SSN that improper use of the number is a constant worry. "Your Social Security number was never meant to serve the various functions it is used for today," writes Robert Siciliano, head of IDTheftSecurity.com. "But 'functionality creep,' which occurs when an item, process, or procedure ends up serving a purpose it was never intended to perform, soon took effect. . . . All this leads up to the unfortunate realization that your Social Security number is out there in hundreds, or even thou-

> "Your Social Security number is out there in hundreds, or even thousands of places. It is most definitely not private, nor can it be adequately protected."[7]
>
> —*Robert Siciliano, head of IDTheftSecurity.com.*

sands of places. It is most definitely not private, nor can it be adequately protected."[7]

Another development that affected individual privacy was the increased use of credit cards. The first credit cards were single-purpose cards used to purchase telegraph service or gasoline. In 1950 the Diners Club card became the first general-purpose credit card. It was designed for use by business people and was affiliated with restaurants, hotels, and car rental agencies. The Diners Club card allowed an individual to charge purchases at a variety of businesses and receive a single monthly statement showing all transactions. Of course, these statements also revealed private information about the user, such as his or her level of spending or particular spending habits. Nevertheless, the ease and convenience of the concept made it wildly successful, and soon other companies were offering their own credit cards. Businesses of all kinds eventually began to accept credit cards, and consumer debt surged to new highs.

Applying for a credit card requires a person to provide name, home address, employer's name and address, and often credit references from other businesses, information that becomes the permanent property of credit card companies. Even before the use of computers to sort and store information, employees at credit card companies began to search for patterns in consumer data, such as which occupations accounted for the most frequent missed payments. The explosion of purchases on credit also led to the rise of credit bureaus that compiled and maintained vast amounts of data about consumers, including purchases of homes and automobiles, bank loans, shopping history, and payment records. A person's credit history was used to compile a credit rating that affected his or her ability to apply for loans or make large purchases on credit. Whatever consumers thought about this potential threat to their privacy, they continued to apply for and use credit cards in record numbers. By the 1980s not only business travelers but also ordinary shoppers often carried multiple credit cards. Today credit cards are so widely used that a popular ad campaign depicted a shopper trying to pay with cash as a misfit who disrupts the smooth procession of swiped-card purchases.

When a person charges items on a credit card, his or her personal information can be gathered and used by companies interested in selling other items.

Personal Computers, the Internet, and Social Media

Probably the largest current conflicts between convenience and privacy concerns are the result of two inventions: the personal computer (PC) and the Internet. The personal computer not only offered a user dozens of software programs to do various tasks, it also enabled the user to connect to other computer networks via phone lines or, later, broadband cable connections. The Internet—also called the World Wide Web—provided a global system of interconnected computer networks, giving people unprecedented access to information and the ability to communicate with others in many ways, including by electronic mail, or e-mail. Users began to "surf the web," or explore websites at random. People searched for like-minded groups of users who had the same interests, hobbies, occupations, or political beliefs. Many were willing to share the most intimate details about themselves through group conversations called chat rooms or on online dating sites. Users became increasingly comfortable making online financial transactions that called for personal information such as a credit card number, address, and phone number.

The Internet also offered vast new opportunities for data mining by organizations and businesses. Google, the best-known and most frequently used search engine online, collects and stores information about individual searches, enabling the company to provide sponsored ads that are keyed to certain words and pop up during a search. Small bits of data called cookies are stored on a user's hard drive when she or he visits certain websites, which allows a business to deliver targeted ads to that user. Navigating the Internet today means being followed incessantly by ads and offers linked to whatever topic or product one is pursuing. A person's online activity can be tracked by the person's Internet service provider (ISP), by the servers that connect the person's browser to websites, and by the websites themselves, providing a detailed history of online usage. The notion of surfing the web anonymously in the privacy of one's home can be a dangerous illusion.

Another threat to privacy is the rise of social media. Facebook, LinkedIn, YouTube, Instagram, and Twitter are among the social media sites on which users share all kinds of information, some of it extremely personal. Facebook, a social networking site founded in 2004, has exploded in popularity with more than 1 billion users worldwide. On the site users post personal profiles, share articles, photographs, and videos, and often provide up-to-the-minute information about where they are and what they are doing. Twitter,

The Permanence of Electronic Data

When thinking about the Internet, most people focus on its immediacy—how it allows for instantaneous sharing of information. Yet just as important to an individual's online privacy is the fact of data permanence. Rapid growth of storage capabilities means that data, once uploaded to the web, generally remains there unchanged, available to whoever tries to access it later. In short, what goes online stays online. Of course, data can be deleted, but even then there is a chance that someone has already copied the information or shared it with others. "Most of the stuff on the web is living on a hard drive somewhere, and it doesn't cost a whole lot to store," says Eric Tornoe, a computer security expert at the University of St. Thomas in St. Paul, Minnesota. "When you erase a disk drive, that data is still almost as easy to get back as it is if you haven't erased the drive. [Experts] don't consider anything truly secure unless you physically destroy the drive."

Data permanence can be a particular problem for younger people, who often are more liberal about what they are willing to post and share on the web. Embarrassing photographs, videos, or self-revealing posts can hide in the digital thicket for months or years, just waiting to be discovered by a college admissions worker or potential employer. The vastness of the Internet can make it seem unlikely that old information will turn up again in an unpleasant context, but the chance is always there.

Quoted in Nichelle Heu, "Digital Permanence: What Goes on the Internet Stays on the Internet," *ThreeSixty*, July 3, 2013. www.threesixtyjournalism.org.

another hugely popular social media site that began in 2006, enables users to exchange and distribute 140-character text messages called tweets. With laptop computers, cellular smart phones, and tablets, individuals can post on social media from almost anywhere. The immediacy of these sites has made them important sources of breaking news and of public reactions to unfolding events. Yet many critics bemoan the way users willingly surrender their privacy and even become exhibitionists online. "Every time you post an update to Facebook," writes Susan Krauss Whitbourne, a professor of psychology at the University of Massachusetts–Amherst, "think very hard about the image you're communicating and whether this is the image that will get you closer to achieving your life goals. You might also question your own motives. Ask yourself why you feel this need to share, or perhaps overshare, the details of your personal life."[8] As social media continue to gain popularity, the debate about privacy will surely continue as well. Everyone should be aware of how personal information can be misused or exploited by unscrupulous people who troll the Internet.

Chapter 2

How Hackers Operate

In March 2014 visitors to the website of computer game maker Electronic Arts (EA) were confronted with a log-in screen headed "My Apple ID." The site looked like a typical page used to link to various Apple services, such as iTunes and Apple's online store. The screen prompted visitors to sign in using their Apple ID and password. Then a second screen asked for the user's full name, credit card number, date of birth, phone number, and other information. Once these details were submitted, the user was transferred to a genuine Apple ID site. The fake log-in screens proved to be part of an elaborate trick to get EA's customers to reveal personal information to an unknown third party. Alerted to the scam by workers at Netcraft, an Internet security firm, EA immediately blocked access to the screens. The company did not say how many people, if any, had been tricked into revealing sensitive information, but the security breach was potentially serious. Apparently a computer hacker took advantage of old software to enter EA's network through a calendar application. "The mere presence of old software can often provide sufficient incentive for a hacker to target one system over another, and to spend more time looking for additional vulnerabilities or trying to probe deeper into the internal network,"[9] according to a spokesperson from Netcraft. The cyberattack marked the second time EA's servers had been attacked in 2014. This latest incident seemed puzzling and rather clumsy to experts, since EA has few business links to Apple. Nevertheless, EA felt it necessary to reassure its customers that its website was safe and secure.

Skills and Expertise of Hackers

The EA incident was the work of a computer hacker—a person who seeks weaknesses in a computer network in order to gain illegal access to data. The term *hacker* is said to have originated in the 1960s at the

Massachusetts Institute of Technology (MIT), where it was used to refer to a student who avoided the ordinary channels of study and followed his or her own approach to learning. Many current dictionaries still include a definition of hackers as programming experts who solve problems with computers and search for new and innovative ways to use them. Over time, however, the term has come to refer to someone who breaks in to computer websites or networks with malicious intent. A hacker wants to steal, change, or destroy information. In other words, he or she is a cybercriminal.

Hackers have certain skills and expertise that enable them to break in to online systems and gain access to personal information. First, they learn how to program by acquiring different computer languages, such as Python or Perl. Experienced hackers generally can learn a new computer language in days by relating what's in a manual to what they already know. They are well practiced at reading and writing code. Second, hackers are expert at using Unix, a family of open-source computer operating systems that are basic to the function of the Internet. "Open-source" means that the software can be used, modified, and distributed by anyone. This is in contrast to Microsoft's or Apple's "closed-source" operating systems, consisting of codes that cannot be read or modified. Expertise with Unix-related systems such as Linux helps hackers tap into websites and networks on the web. Hackers also know basic HyperText Markup Language (HTML), which is the code for all the pictures, graphics, and design components on a website. Hackers can use this skill for "phishing," or creating fake screens or sites like the ones on the EA network. Finally, hackers often have the ability to think outside the box and identify vulnerable spots in networks. The imagination on which legitimate programmers pride themselves in their work is also seen in successful cybercriminals.

In recent years expertise and imagination have become less essential for aspiring hackers. There are now software programs available for hackers that are like virtual do-it-yourself tool kits for cracking into networks. A typical program enables hackers to select from a list of software vulnerabilities they might want to exploit in order to infiltrate a website or network. Graphics such as bar graphs and tables help hackers keep track of how many operating systems and browsers

Online sites such as iTunes have allowed hackers opportunities to gather information that can be used to steal identities or commit other fraudulent acts.

they have breached and in which countries. Such programs provide criminal opportunities for hackers who are far from being experts. For example, in 2010 three Spanish hackers infiltrated a network of almost 13 million computers in 190 countries using a web-based botnet program, which allows attackers to seize control of affected computers. "These people didn't have any advanced hacker skills," says Sean-Paul Correll, a researcher at Panda Security, which investigated the scheme. "They just had resources available to them online and were able to take advantage of them to build a network."[10] Ominously for Internet users, the number of web-based data-stealing programs available to hackers continues to grow.

Information That Hackers Seek

Just as important to Internet users is the kind of personal information that hackers seek to steal. Most hackers want information that can be used immediately for financial gain, such as the following:

- User names, passwords, and PINs
- Social Security numbers
- Phone, utility, and cable account numbers
- Bank and credit card account numbers
- Insurance ID numbers
- Driver's license number
- Passport number
- Employment and student ID numbers
- College financial-aid information

Hackers use these numbers and data for identity theft, which is the use of an individual's personal information to commit fraud. Hackers can use credit card numbers to make purchases themselves or sell the numbers to a third party. A single number can be sold for ten to fifty dollars, while the number of a no-limit elite card owned by a consumer with good credit is worth hundreds of dollars. Therefore a hacker who breaks in to a large company's network to steal thousands or even millions of card numbers can potentially make very large sums. Hackers can also use stolen Social Security and insurance policy numbers to file fraudulent tax returns or make bogus insurance claims. Such crimes can cause victims to spend months or even years trying to clear up tax or credit score problems. Many merchants simply accept such crime as an additional cost of doing business instead of investing in safer systems. Mark Rasch, a cybersecurity specialist and former federal prosecutor, points out that local law enforcement lacks the personnel and expertise to deal with smaller cases of identity crime, while the Federal Bureau of Investigation (FBI) concentrates only on massive data thefts. "Police don't want to be bothered," Rasch says. "It's a difficult crime to investigate, and the feeling is, 'Oh, we're never going to catch these guys.'"[11] As a result, hackers operate with impunity.

> "These people didn't have any advanced hacker skills. They just had resources available to them online and were able to take advantage of them to build a network."[10]
>
> *—Sean-Paul Correll, a researcher at Panda Security who investigated a 2010 scheme by three Spanish hackers.*

Varied Motives for Hacking

As hackers become more numerous, their profiles and motives grow more varied. Most common is the criminal hacker—also called a cracker or black hat hacker—who seeks financial gain from hijacking computer data in any way possible, from identity theft to pirating software. The criminal hacker may work alone, in a small group, or for a large criminal organization making use of his or her expertise. It is estimated that criminal hackers stole more than $20 billion from consumers in 2012.

Another type of hacker is politically motivated. These activist hackers, or "hacktivists," use cyberattacks on governments, corporations, or religious groups in an attempt to make a political point or reveal sensitive information. Hacktivist groups tend to be decentralized, with general goals of attracting publicity by disrupting websites or stealing data from certain high-profile organizations. Often they seek to reveal hidden or potentially embarrassing information, as with Edward Snowden, the American programmer who disclosed sensitive details about the National Security Agency's surveillance program, and the anonymous hacker who exposed stolen e-mails from climate scientists at the University of East Anglia in Norwich, England, that raised questions about the group's claims in its research on global warming.

"Police don't want to be bothered. [Hacking is] a difficult crime to investigate, and the feeling is, 'Oh, we're never going to catch these guys.'"[11]

—Mark Rasch, cybersecurity specialist and former federal prosecutor.

A third type of hacker is the state-sponsored cyberattacker. Supported by governments and thus well funded and especially dangerous, these hackers represent a worrisome recent development. They tend to be talented and clever, employing the most advanced attack code in order to steal state secrets or disrupt government systems. Examples of state-sponsored hacking attacks include Operation Aurora, in which attackers thought to be Chinese gained access to Google and other large companies in order to steal sensitive data, and the Stuxnet incident, in which a Western government—likely

Ethical Hackers

Some computer experts insist that not all hackers are criminals or vandals. An ethical hacker is someone hired to attack a security system on behalf of its owners. He or she probes for vulnerabilities in popular applications and platforms that could be exploited by a malicious hacker. Ethical hackers employ the same techniques as their criminal counterparts but use them to identify system weaknesses so that they can be eliminated. Ethical hackers are sometimes called white hats to differentiate them from the illicit black hats. (In old Western films, cowboy heroes wore white hats, while villains wore black hats.) The first ethical hackers were groups of computer experts called red teams that the federal government hired to test its own computer systems.

Today, with the growing threat from malicious hackers, many large companies maintain their own teams of ethical hackers. Such initiatives have helped ethical hackers gain widespread acceptance. For example, in November 2013 Facebook and Microsoft announced a new policy of paying bounties to hackers who detect vulnerabilities not only in their own products and systems but anywhere in the Internet infrastructure. The companies organized a panel of experts charged with making awards of $5,000 or more to hackers who uncover serious weaknesses. "A lot of hidden bugs survive in very important code," says Dan Kaminsky, cofounder of White Ops, a fraud prevention company. Kaminsky sees bounty payments as "a game changer for protecting users."

Quoted in Byron Acohido, "Ethical 'White Hat' Hackers Play Vital Security Role," *USA Today*, November 11, 2013. www.usatoday.com.

the United States—sabotaged the computer system for Iran's nuclear enrichment facilities, apparently causing extensive damage.

Yet another kind of hacker enjoys showing off his or her computer skills by causing confusion and mayhem. Hackers who commit cybervandalism are usually thrill seekers who delight in disrupting governmental or corporate networks simply for the challenge, with no thought of financial gain or political motive.

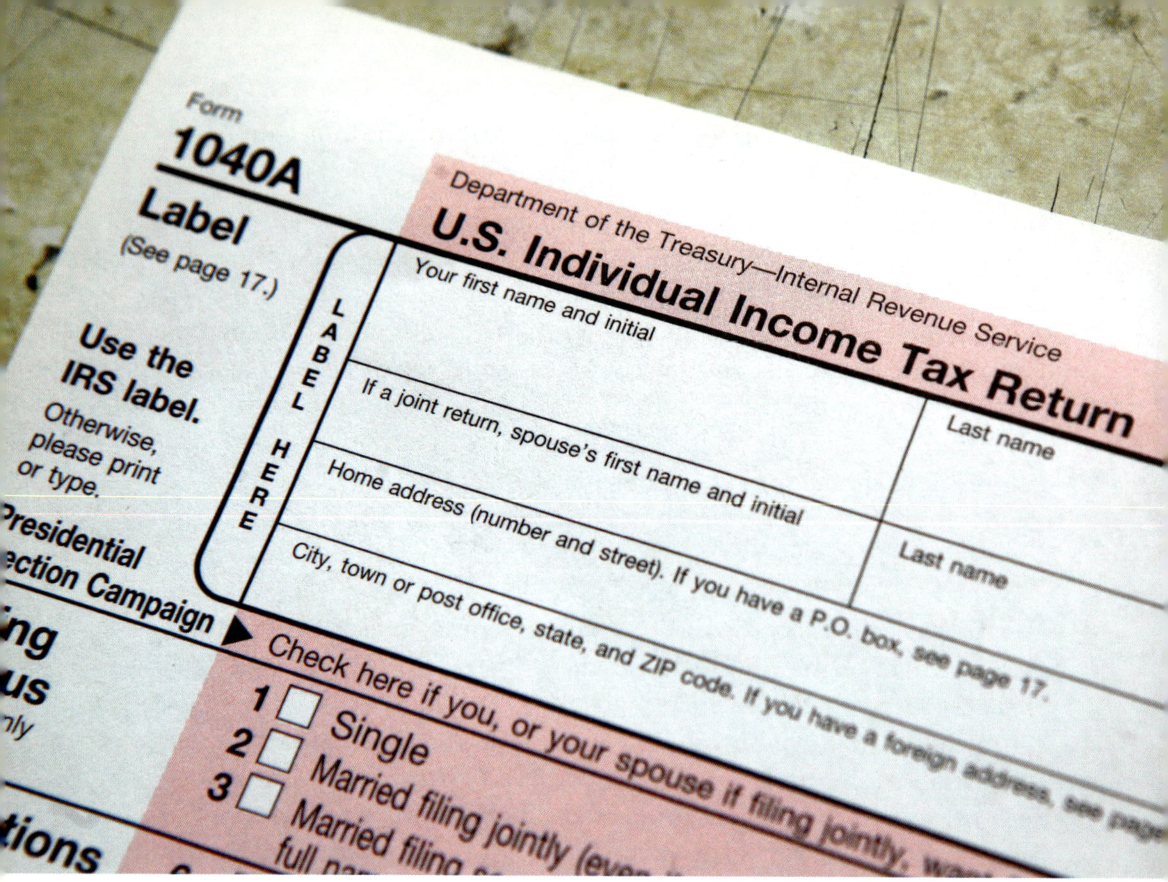

Hackers can use stolen Social Security numbers to file fake tax returns. It can take years for the victims of such scams to get the matter resolved.

A Variety of Hacking Methods

Whatever their motives, hackers employ many different methods to break in to computer systems or steal personal data. One of the most frequently used methods is called phishing. This is a scam that attempts to fool people into offering their personal information or paying a fee. For example, an e-mail might ask for help in smuggling millions out of a foreign country by transferring the money to the recipient's bank account. The help required is the person's bank account number and bank site password. The previously mentioned fake log-in screens on EA's website are another example of a phishing scam. A similar hacking ruse is called bait and switch. This occurs when a user begins to download proper content that is then switched out with some type of malware (short for malicious software) for collecting information. Hackers can set up a bait and switch scam by buying advertising space on popular websites. When visitors click on the ad or try to make a purchase, the innocent link or content changes to something malicious.

Viruses and Malware

A number of hacking schemes involve viruses that infiltrate a computer. A Trojan horse (or simply Trojan) is a virus capable of recording everything a person types and sending it back to the hacker or sending out spam e-mails to attack other computers. The virus may also be time activated, spreading silently for days, months, or years until it activates and does damage on a specific date. Often a Trojan is disguised as a harmless e-mail that informs the user about a problem with a shipping company or bank service. The message urges the user to click on an e-mail attachment, which installs the virus. Another type of Trojan looks like a video posted on Facebook or Twitter. A popup message prompts the reader to click a button to update the video player, which instead downloads the virus. Hackers also use file-name tricks to fool users into thinking they are clicking to see provocative pictures of film stars or other racy material.

Malware used by hackers includes many variations on computer viruses. Worms have the advantage of being network aware, enabling them to seek new hosts on a network and spread more quickly than ordinary viruses. The most ingenious worms can go global in seconds, making them very difficult to control. Spyware infiltrates a computer like a virus does but instead snoops on a user's activity and sends gathered data—such as user names, passwords, and account numbers—back to the hacker. A zombie is a computer infiltrated with malware that does the bidding of a hacker at long distance. A botnet, or zombie army, occurs when a number of computers on the Internet are co-opted as zombies and reprogrammed to steal data or overload transmissions on a commercial website. Many experts think botnets are the largest threat to the Internet today. Hackers also probe for vulnerabilities in website frameworks in order to introduce a virus that can spread quickly. An infected website can spread malware to all the computers that visit the site. Even when an infected website is restored, the damage to a company's reputation and trustworthiness can be disastrous. Hackers also attack websites by engaging in cookie theft. That is when a hacker steals a user's cookie—the small text file sent to a user's computer by a website in order to track visits. With a stolen cookie, the hacker can navigate a website as if he or she had supplied the victim's log-on name and password.

The growth of Wi-Fi networks, or wireless networks, for transmitting computer data provides hackers with more opportunities. Hackers can hijack a supposedly closed Wi-Fi network from outside, enabling them to see and record what a user is typing on a computer. A Wi-Fi network, which provides Internet connection through radio waves, can originate from a home, office, or restaurant and is vulnerable to hackers when access is not encrypted with a password. Some hackers also set up fake wireless networks. They can label them with the name of an airport or restaurant in an attempt to fool users into logging on and inadvertently giving up personal information.

No doubt hackers will continue to invent ways to infiltrate computer networks. Computer security expert Roger A. Grimes warns

Governments are no strangers to hacking. The US government was thought to have hacked into Iran's nuclear reactor facilities (shown) to fatally shut down the system.

users to be wary of hackers. "When a hacker modifies your system in a stealthy way, it isn't your system anymore—it belongs to the hackers," says Grimes. "What you think is a clean system and what really is a clean system may all be controlled by the wily hacker."[12]

Staying Anonymous

One measure of a hacker's cleverness is the ability to maintain anonymity on the Internet. In fact, one shadowy group of activist hackers based in London actually called themselves Anonymous. The group, which launched attacks on PayPal, Visa, and MasterCard, among many other sites, used a number of different techniques to avoid detection. One advantage they had in common with everyone who uses the Internet is that IP addresses, which are assigned to every online user, expire very quickly—usually as soon as someone disconnects. A person's next connection receives a new IP address, making each user very difficult to track. In addition, law enforcement officers have to get a warrant to investigate the service provider for a specific IP address. For a global operation like Anonymous, investigators had to deal with multiple jurisdictions, making their job that much more difficult.

> "When a hacker modifies your system in a stealthy way, it isn't your system anymore—it belongs to the hackers. . . . What you think is a clean system and what really is a clean system may all be controlled by the wily hacker."[12]
>
> *—Roger A. Grimes, computer security expert.*

Hackers also hide their tracks by using proxy servers. These are servers that are located far from a user's computer or that maintain no records of where activity originates, or sometimes both. Proxies are popular for doing illegal downloads or sending messages in countries with hostile regimes. They are also invaluable to criminal hackers. Another technique is onion routing, which was originally developed by the US Navy for untraceable online communication. Onion routing programs are freely available and run on most operating systems. They create Internet connections that resist traffic analysis and eavesdropping.

Hackers Who Blackmail

Increasingly hackers are using blackmail as another method of profiting from their skills. Like terrorists or kidnappers, hackers rely on fear and intimidation to extort cash from victims, in essence asking companies to pay them not to steal their data or crash their websites. Statistics on this form of cybercrime are hard to find because companies do not want to admit they have paid ransoms and thus encourage more blackmail. Nevertheless, one web security firm estimates that hackers extort more than $5 million from their victims each year. And apparently the problem is growing.

In a typical blackmail attack, a hacker will knock a victim's website offline for several minutes. Then the hacker will bring the site back online and send an e-mail demanding a wired payment to prevent another attack. Most companies prefer to pay quietly rather than face continuing disruption. While most cyberblackmailers settle for a few hundred dollars, some are more ambitious. In 2012 a Hungarian hacker stole data from computers of the Marriott Hotel chain and threatened to reveal embarrassing information unless Marriott gave him a $150,000 job and other perks. Another hacker walled off patient records from a doctor's office and demanded $50,000 to restore them. Experts urge victims to contact law enforcement instead of paying the blackmailers. "I've never heard of a company actually surviving a cyber extortion by paying the money," says James Aquilina, a former federal cybercrime prosecutor. "It just delays the inevitable. It doesn't make it go away."

Quoted in Gerry Smith, "Forget Stealing Credit Cards, Now Hackers Just Straight-Up Blackmail You," *Huffington Post*, March 28, 2014. www.huffingtonpost.com.

With these sophisticated tricks at their disposal, hackers such as the ones in Anonymous often become overconfident. Investigators discovered online forums where the Anonymous hackers would discuss their latest targets and boast about successful attacks. This led to their arrest and conviction for damaging the websites of several multinational businesses. Peter Testar, the judge who sentenced the hackers, says, "The defendants were actually rather arrogant. They thought they were far too clever to be caught and used various methods to try to cloak and preserve their anonymity. It seems to me that the police were a little bit more clever than the conspirators."[13]

The battle between hackers and law enforcement is ongoing, with millions or even billions of dollars at stake, not to mention sensitive information that is vital to countries' national security. Such efforts can seem far removed from an ordinary computer user, but in reality the dangers involved are always just one click away.

Chapter 3

Hacking and Identity Theft

In April 2013 Kellie Droste, a speech therapist from Maricopa, Arizona, learned from her accountant that her husband's and her joint tax return could not be filed because a hacker had already filed a federal return using her Social Security number. The problem took months to sort out and caused a delay in the couple's $2,700 tax refund. In August Droste received a call from a Discover card customer service representative requesting more information about her recent credit card application. Droste explained that she had not applied for a Discover card. Someone had made the application using her name, date of birth, and Social Security number. Droste had to spend hours on the phone trying to resolve the matter and prevent further fraudulent uses of her personal information. She even filed a police report on the incident and provided Phoenix police with an address from the bogus application in the hope it would lead to the hacker or hackers behind it. However, the police said there was little they could do. Recent data from the Federal Trade Commission shows that Arizona has more victims of identity theft per capita than any other state. Yet Phoenix, Arizona, law-enforcement officials admit that it is very difficult to catch hackers who steal personal data for gain, as in Droste's case. The hackers generally use fake addresses and phone numbers along with the genuine stolen data in order to foil investigators. The result is increasing consumer uneasiness about identity theft and frustration because the perpetrators so rarely are caught.

A Rapidly Growing Crime

Identity theft is the fastest-growing crime in the United States and is also on the rise globally. Government agencies and private firms spend huge amounts to combat potential hackers and identity thieves. As privacy expert Frederick S. Lane writes:

> The modern-day epidemic of identity theft stems from the toxic combination of an intrinsically insecure Social Security number that has become a de facto national identification number, massive computer databases vulnerable to hacking, a rapidly growing global data and communications network, and lax security procedures that allow databases and data processing reports to be stored on laptops. . . . With the right information, an identity thief can empty bank accounts, max out credit cards, open new credit card accounts (and max out those as well), take out loans, and then simply disappear, leaving the victim to struggle for months or years to reestablish his or her true identity.[14]

"With the right information, an identity thief can empty bank accounts, max out credit cards, open new credit card accounts (and max out those as well), take out loans, and then simply disappear, leaving the victim to struggle for months or years to reestablish his or her true identity."[14]

—*Privacy expert Frederick S. Lane.*

Not surprisingly, hackers' tools for identity theft are also proliferating. The number of malware programs designed to steal personal information has grown from about 1 million in 2007 to more than 130 million today. Many of these programs are installed covertly on computers and then proceed to complete an array of secret operations without the user's permission. As the programs grow more sophisticated, they require less expertise on the part of hackers. Some malware programs provide running tallies of hacked accounts and locations, enabling hackers to keep track of their crimes and stay one step ahead of investigators. Sites on the Internet offer lists of malware and detailed advice on different methods for stealing personal information. One website features a thorough listing of the different places where identity thieves can access personal data, some of which—such as trash cans—require no hacking whatsoever.

Having one's identity stolen can result in years of disputes with companies and hours of frustrating time on the phone.

With hacking and identity theft so common today, government agencies and private businesses are constantly working to improve their data security. Authorities also strive to inform people how they can better protect their personal information online. Yet hackers are always finding new ways to profit from identity theft. In March 2014 three members of an alleged cybercrime group were arrested in San Francisco for hacking customer accounts at several large financial companies, including JPMorgan Chase Bank. The trio intended to steal $15 million in customer deposits by intercepting log-in data from company accounts and moving victims' money to fraudulent accounts created by the conspirators. The fake accounts could then be emptied through ATM withdrawals or debit card purchases. Not stopping there, the thieves also intended to file bogus tax returns in the names of their identity theft victims, funneling tax refunds into the fake accounts. Online brokerage firms have also seen a rise in hacker attacks and identity theft involving their customers' accounts. Another new wrinkle appeared when a ring of hackers in Vancouver, Canada, sought to steal the loyalty reward points from victims' credit card accounts. Seemingly no accounts or customer benefits are safe from these schemes.

Obtaining Social Security Numbers

The focus of many identity theft hacking schemes is the Social Security number—or its equivalent in other nations with social welfare programs. As mentioned, a person's SSN has become practically a national ID number, keyed for better or worse to all sorts of personal information about an individual. "A Social Security number is like a skeleton key—able to unlock a kingdom of untold riches for identity thieves," writes Adam Levin, former director of the New Jersey Division of Consumer Affairs. "It is the central piece of data needed to hijack our credit, steal our health insurance, use us as human shields and generally wreak havoc in our lives."[15] Levin and other critics point out that government mismanagement of SSNs can put citizens' identities at risk—and sometimes even their safety. Experts insist that SSNs are much too easily obtainable on the Internet and elsewhere. For example, SSNs frequently appear on the Internet in court records or documents from government agencies. Medicare cards, which the US government instructs individuals to carry at all times when away from home, are each stamped with the bearer's SSN, making it prey to muggers and pickpockets. Tax forms at all levels of government also prominently feature SSNs.

> "A Social Security number is like a skeleton key—able to unlock a kingdom of untold riches for identity thieves. It is the central piece of data needed to hijack our credit, steal our health insurance, use us as human shields and generally wreak havoc in our lives."[15]
>
> *—Adam Levin, former director of the New Jersey Division of Consumer Affairs.*

Many private companies use SSNs for filing and for tracking customers, which can play into the hands of determined hackers. Lists of SSNs are sometimes obtained from stolen laptop computers or flash drives, or simply by rummaging through trash containers outside careless firms. Security experts say that hackers can also deduce most of the numbers in a SSN using publicly available information. Hackers know that SSNs have been issued in a pattern. The first three numbers indicate the state where the person lived when the number was assigned. The two middle numbers and the last four numbers were also assigned sequentially. The Social Security Administration also keeps a Death Master File (publicly available for a fee) that records the deaths of Americans along with their SSN, birth date, and death date. With this data and information about when and where a person was born, hackers can narrow down the possibilities for the remaining SSN numbers and find them with a "brute force attack" that rapidly tries various combinations. According to Alessandro Acquisti and Ralph Grossy, researchers who have studied the confidentiality of SSNs, "If one can successfully identify all nine digits of a SSN in fewer than 10, 100 or even 1,000 attempts, that Social Security number is no more secure than a three-digit PIN."[16] To address this problem, the Social Security Administration began assigning SSNs randomly in 2011. Doubtless hackers will search for hidden patterns in the new assignments as well as use other methods to obtain SSNs.

Meanwhile, number theft continues. In 2013 investigators discovered an illicit online service selling SSNs, birth records, and credit and background reports on millions of Americans, including public figures such as First Lady Michelle Obama, CIA director John Brennan, and entertainers Beyoncé, Jay-Z, and Kanye West. The information had been hacked from some of the largest consumer and business data firms in the United States, including Dun & Bradstreet. In February 2014 hackers stole more than three hundred thousand student SSNs from a database at the University of Maryland. Regardless of how they are accumulated, SSNs are coveted by hackers as a crucial component of identity theft.

Hacking Credit Card Numbers and Financial Data

Another category of data that identity thieves seek is credit card numbers and numbers of financial accounts. When victims open their financial statements and notice bogus charges or withdrawals,

Celebrities such as Jay-Z and Beyoncé can also be the victims of identity theft.

they wonder how their card numbers or bank accounts were compromised. Actually, hackers have a variety of methods from which to choose. Some might hack companies' web commerce systems, where customers' credit card information is stored to make repeated purchases easier to complete. Even if a company's database of credit card numbers and other personal information is encrypted, the hacker can sometimes probe for security flaws to bypass the safeguard and gather large numbers of cards instantly. Hackers can place devices called skimmers on automatic teller machines (ATMs) or card readers on gas pumps. When a customer inserts his or her card into the reader, it also passes through the skimmer, enabling it to record the account data. Hackers have even used Wi-Fi-equipped laptops to perpetrate drive-by hacks of retailers' computer networks. For example, in 2005 a small band of hackers used this method to download database files from the central servers of TJX, the parent company of retail outlets such as Marshalls and T.J. Maxx. While parked in the lot outside a Marshalls store in St. Paul, Minnesota, the team pointed a telescope-shaped antenna at the store and tapped into its Wi-Fi to decode data streaming between hand-held price-check devices, cash registers, and the store's computers. The hackers then managed to reach the central TJX database and download millions of credit card numbers, as well as SSNs and driver's license numbers for 450,000 TJX customers. The hack went undetected for more than a year and ended up costing TJX $250 million, including lawsuit settlements. Moreover, it led to demands that companies do more to secure their data.

Hackers also employ various phishing schemes. In one ploy, the hacker calls someone at work, pretends to be an employee of the person's

Retail chains such as TJ Maxx have been victimized by hackers using Wi-Fi to download hundreds of credit card, Social Security, and driver's license numbers.

Child Identity Theft

For a hacker it is often more desirable to steal a child's personal information than an adult's. While the average adult pays bills regularly and monitors financial transactions via bank statements, credit card statements, and credit reports, a child has no reason to use his or her Social Security number. Children are not old enough to apply for credit or loans and cannot open a bank account without a parent or guardian's signature. As a result an identity thief can use a child's personal information, secure in the likelihood that no one will be checking any financial transactions associated with that data. Thus a case of child identity theft can go on for months or even years before anyone notices a delinquent loan or plummeting credit score. Sometimes parents discover the scam only after pre-approved credit offers in the child's name start arriving in the mail. "The truth is that there's no way for a lender to check on the age attached to an SSN," writes Matt Davis, director of Business Alliances at the Identity Theft Resources Center. "All they can see is the number, the credit history, and a name. If someone is able to successfully forge documentation and has all the right information, they will be able to acquire credit, even if the SSN is supposed to belong to a minor." One thing concerned parents can do is write to the three credit reporting agencies to determine if credit reports linked to their child's SSN exist.

Matt Davis, "Child Identity Theft: The Basics," Identity Theft Resource Center, September 9, 2013. www.idtheftcenter.org.

bank or brokerage, and tricks the person into revealing card numbers or account numbers. Other phishing schemes use fake e-mails and websites to trick individuals into giving up important numbers. For example, an e-mail claiming to be from the recipient's bank might urge the person to log in to the bank's site through a fake link in order to clear up some imaginary problem. The hacker then steals the person's account information through a bogus bank site that the hacker has prepared. Of course identity thieves can often find credit card numbers and bank account numbers in discarded statements or other documents in trash cans. To prevent this kind of theft, more banks and credit card companies are printing only partial numbers on statements and also urging customers to pay bills online to avoid paper statements altogether.

Methods of Using Data for Identity Theft

Despite the efforts of law enforcement and financial companies to stop them, hackers profit from the data they steal in many different ways. Often a hacker will use stolen information such as SSNs to apply for large lines of credit, building up mountains of debt linked to the numbers. Bad debt due to hacking attacks can take years for a victim to resolve and can sometimes lead to bankruptcy. As methods of detection improve, some hackers settle for smaller, more rapid transactions using stolen data. For example, making a $50 charge on each of one thousand hacked credit cards can still result in $50,000 of ill-gotten merchandise or services. Data about the cardholder's state, city, and zip code makes a stolen credit card number even more valuable to hackers. The criminals can create "spoofed," or fraudulent, versions of the victims' cards for use in the immediate vicinity. Utilizing stolen card numbers closer to the area where they were obtained generally enables identity thieves to use the numbers for a longer period before banks or card companies become suspicious and put a hold on the cards. Security analyst Avivah Litan sees this as a worrisome new trend. "It's very significant because it shows how sophisticated the criminals are," says Litan. "They are trying to avoid being spotted by fraud detection systems that check the location of a transaction against the individual's home zip code and the location of that individual's most recent transactions."[17]

"[Using stolen credit cards close to where they were obtained is] very significant because it shows how sophisticated the criminals are. They are trying to avoid being spotted by fraud detection systems that check the location of a transaction against the individual's home zip code and the location of that individual's most recent transactions."[17]

—Security analyst Avivah Litan.

Black Markets for Hackers

The personal information hackers obtain through identity theft is often sold through online black markets, which are illicit exchanges for stolen data. A March 2014 RAND Corporation report on these black markets reveals that they have grown into a multibillion dollar economy displaying unprecedented levels of sophistication. The RAND report describes the markets as well organized, carefully policed (by criminals), and subject to strict rules. "Shoppers" can purchase stolen data such as credit card numbers, SSNs, and birth dates as well as tools for cybercrime such as malware and instructions on how to conduct a hacking attack. According to RAND, botnets used to launch a Distributed Denial of Service (DDoS) attack are available for fifty dollars for a twenty-four-hour attack. Those who fail to provide the goods or services they advertise are quickly expelled. Illicit "storefronts" conduct e-commerce much like legitimate websites and include chat rooms, instant messaging channels, and forums for hackers. Transactions in these cyber–black markets often are conducted with virtual currencies such as Bitcoin that are difficult to trace due to their security profile and anonymity. "The [cyber] black market can be more profitable than the illegal drug trade," write the authors of the report. "Links to end-users are more direct, and because worldwide distribution is accomplished electronically, the requirements are negligible." In other words, the report merely confirms what other researchers have indicated: Hacking as a business is exploding.

Lillian Ablon, Martin C. Libicki, and Andrea A. Golay, "Markets for Cybercrime Tools and Stolen Data," RAND Corporation, 2014. www.rand.org.

Another popular identity theft scheme is to use SSNs to create fraudulent tax returns claiming large tax refunds. A hacker might establish a bogus bank account for the purpose of receiving the refunds, then empty the account and promptly close it. With federal tax refunds now provided on debit cards, hackers can forgo creating a bank account and simply make purchases or cash out the card at a series of

ATMs. Hackers also use stolen employment files from private companies to get employer ID numbers (EINs) and create bogus W-2 forms. These enable the hackers to report fictitious income and withheld taxes to the Internal Revenue Service, which aids in filing fraudulent tax forms. Such schemes can cause businesses and employees to spend enormous amounts of time—and money for accountants' and attorneys' fees—to reconcile with the IRS.

Hackers recently have taken advantage of the economic downturn to set up debt elimination schemes. Cyberthieves search databases for individuals who have high mortgage loan or credit card debt and ply them with mailings that promise a path to paying off the debt for a fraction of the original amount. To take advantage of the deal, the individual must pay a fee of $1,500 or more up front and provide sensitive financial information to the bogus company. The participant must also pay a percentage of the satisfied debt to the company. As a result, the hacker not only gets cash but personal numbers that can lead to more illegal profits.

There have even been cases of identity theft rings using stolen personal information to apply for money from federal student loan programs. In 2011 a seventy-one-year-old teaching coordinator named Christina Benson received a visit from a representative of the US Department of Education looking into fraudulent federal student loan applications. Benson learned that hackers had used her personal data to receive federal funding to attend two online community colleges. After deducting tuition and fees, the schools passed the remainder of the loans to the fake "student," providing the hackers with a healthy profit. After a year spent trying to clear her name, Benson received help from Vicki Volkert, an investigator for a fraud prevention company. Volkert points out that online schools provide opportunities for identity thieves. "Traditionally, a student would present herself to the student aid and college registration office, she'd get a photo ID, and then be cleared to attend college," says Volkert. "When it's all online they don't do any of that. There's no verification of your identity with these online schools."[18]

Whatever their methods, hackers continue to profit from identity theft. In the process they also spread uneasiness among the public about the security of personal information and the wisdom of sharing it online.

Chapter 4

Hacking Personal Health Information

Health data is proving to be another area of personal information that is prey to hacking attacks. In January 2014 officials at Ohio Edgepark Medical Supplies discovered a breach in the company's server going back nine months. Hackers had broken in via software used to run the Twinsburg, Ohio, company's website. Once they had gained access to the company's server, the hackers installed malware that intercepted log-in data for forty-two hundred patients. The stolen data enabled the hackers to see information that included names, dates of birth, medical diagnoses, order history for medical supplies, and phone numbers. One hundred twenty-six patients had their full credit card numbers and expiration dates exposed. AssuraMed, Edgepark's parent company, blamed the breach on antivirus software that failed to detect the hacker's malware. In a letter to affected customers, Cindy Sackett, AssuraMed's vice president in charge of compliance and privacy, apologized for the breach and advised individuals on ways to secure their personal data. "We take the protection of your personal information very seriously," wrote Sackett, "and have taken steps to prevent a similar occurrence, including resetting your account password and removing the malware."[19] Experts point to the Edgepark incident as an example of the dangers associated with putting health care records online. They emphasize that data protection is crucial if patients are to have confidence that their digital records are safe from hackers.

Vulnerability of Digital Health Care Data

Public confidence in the security of electronic medical records may also have been shaken by other recent stories of data breaches. In February 2014 a serious hacking attack was discovered at the five-hospital

St. Joseph Health System in Bryan, Texas. Hackers gained unauthorized access to a St. Joseph server containing personal information for 405,000 patients, including Social Security numbers, dates of birth, addresses, and medical files. Officials traced the attack to IP addresses in China, among other locations. The attack on St. Joseph was the largest data-hacking breach in the health care industry since March 2012, when hackers operating out of eastern Europe accessed the medical records of 780,000 individuals at the Utah Department of Health. There are also disquieting signs that health care groups are failing to protect digital records sufficiently. In May 2014 Boston Medical Center fired a subcontracting vendor after officials at the teaching hospital discovered that health records and personal data for fifteen thousand patients were left unprotected with no password on the vendor's website. This episode demonstrated why more than 70 percent of health care groups say they lack confidence in the ability of third-party vendors to detect data breaches, according to a survey on data security by the Ponemon Institute, which does independent research on privacy and data protection.

"We take the protection of your personal information very seriously, and have taken steps to prevent a similar occurrence, including resetting your account password and removing the malware."[19]

—Cindy Sackett, vice president in charge of compliance and privacy for AssuraMed, in a letter to customers whose personal information was accessed by hackers.

Hackers also benefit from careless individuals and rogue data thieves working at hospitals and clinics. Two incidents from 2012 at Howard University Hospital are typical. In one a thief stole a personal laptop on which a hospital contractor had downloaded more than thirty-four thousand patient files. (Research suggests that 40 percent of health care data breaches involve portable devices such as laptops and hard drives.) The files, which contained not only numbers such as SSNs but also sensitive information related to patient diagnoses, were unencrypted and protected by only a single password. A few weeks later federal prosecutors charged a medical technician at Howard with compiling names, addresses, and Medicare numbers of patients and selling them online. A third incident occurred in Virginia, where military health insurer Tricare announced that backup computer tapes containing medical records of more than 5 million patients were stolen from a contractor.

Reporting rules adopted in 2009 by the Department of Health and Human Services (HHS) require that breaches of medical data affecting more than five hundred patients be reported not only to HHS but to the public. There is also a privacy rule that provides federal protections for individuals' health information, making it a federal offense to steal such data or access it without proper authorization. These federal rules have led to the public being much better informed about issues relating to the privacy of personal health care data and the significant problems with health care data security. At the same time, high profile failures like those previously mentioned have placed HHS in a difficult position. While the agency urges hospitals and doctors to adopt electronic health records, it also punishes providers whose lax security leads to breaches of patients' files. "Mistakes happen, incidents happen, corners get cut from time to time," says Susan McAndrew, deputy director for health information at HHS's

As hospitals become increasingly computerized, the organizations may not be savvy about protecting their patients' health records.

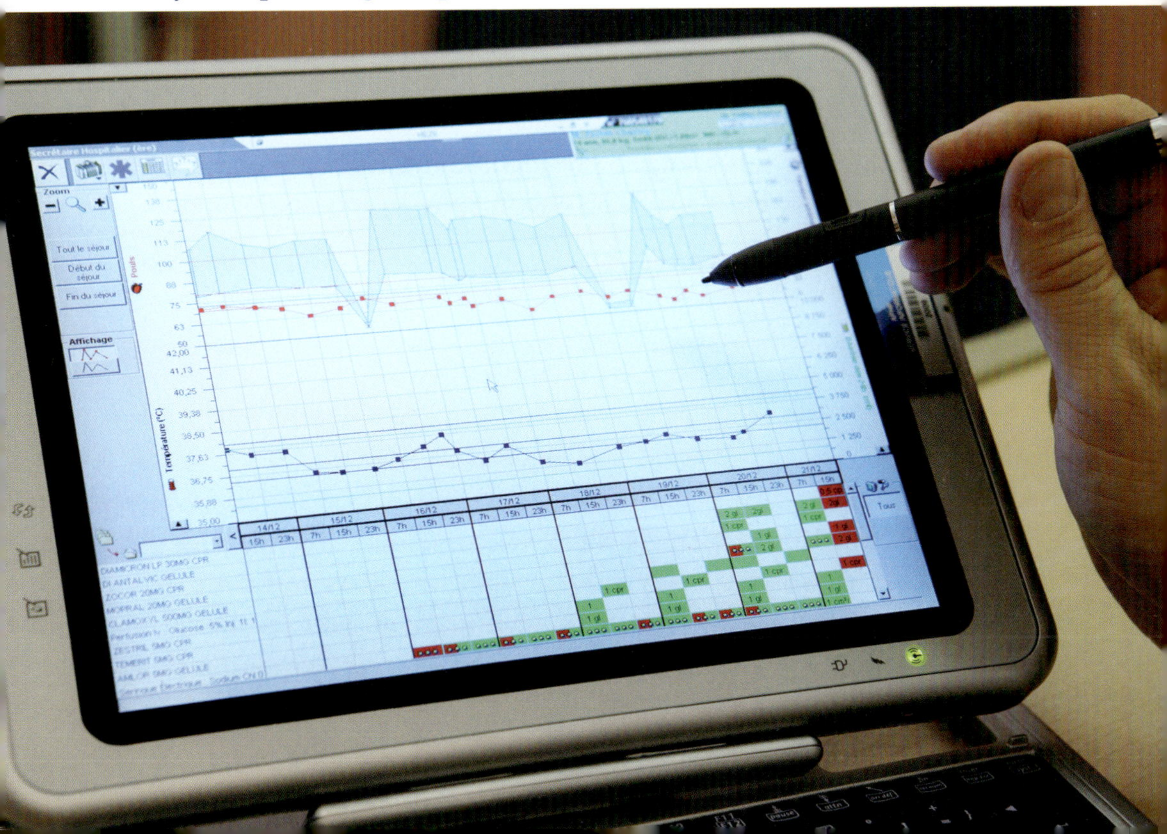

Federal Laws Addressing Confidentiality of Medical Records

Two key federal laws cover the security and confidentiality of medical records. The Health Insurance Portability and Accountability Act (HIPAA), originally passed in 1996, includes federal privacy standards to protect personal health information, particularly in the face of changing electronic technology. The Health Information Technology for Economic and Clinical Health Act (HITECH), enacted in 2009 as part of the Obama administration's legislative package for economic stimulus, was designed to promote electronic sharing of health data by strengthening civil and criminal enforcement of HIPAA rules. Together these laws detail what health care providers and related businesses must do to protect patient records from hackers.

With data breaches increasing, the HHS Office of Civil Rights has stepped up enforcement of HIPAA and HITECH rules. The reporting threshold for the health care industry has been lowered from a "risk of harm" to "probability of compromise" standard. This means that hospitals, clinics, and pharmacies must report more incidents of unauthorized data access and likely will face harsher penalties for leaving data unprotected. Every breach has to be reported directly to the patient or patients affected. If more than five hundred patients are involved, HHS must be informed at once, as well as major local media outlets such as radio, television, and newspapers. "It is not going to help your image to be on the six o'clock news explaining why you lost patient data," says Jeff Hedges, president and CEO of a health care compliance service for pharmacies and medical supply companies.

Quoted in Fred Gebhart, "New HIPAA Requirements Coming," *Drug Topics*, August 15, 2013. http://drugtopics.modernmedicine.com.

Office of Civil Rights. "That's where we come in."[20] To shore up the system HHS has levied heavy fines on some offenders, but critics still insist the problem is growing and that enforcement policies should be tougher.

Why Hackers Seek Medical Records

The hacking of medical records is growing more frequent as hospitals, clinics, and doctor's offices move to electronic protected health information (ePHI). In the past, unauthorized access to ePHI was mostly inadvertent, caused by lax data security or the theft of devices that happened to contain sensitive files. Today, however, hackers are deliberately targeting electronic medical files. One reason that hackers see ePHI as an attractive target is the high prices they can charge buyers of the stolen medical data. For example, while a stolen SSN or credit card number can yield from a few pennies to a few dollars profit on data exchanges, medical information typically brings a profit of as much as $50 per record. Such lucrative potential has resulted in health care data theft more than doubling in frequency between 2003 and 2012. In 2013 alone more than 2 million individuals were victims of health care data theft.

Hackers and those who purchase hacked medical data through online black markets can use it to perpetrate a new kind of identity theft. They can gain fraudulent access to medical treatments, prescription drugs, and insurance payments. The victims may be wealthy individuals with gold-plated insurance plans, like the federal judge in Florida whose medical identity was hacked and used to file false insurance claims for two prosthetic legs. They are just as likely to be ordinary individuals whose Medicare or Medicaid numbers are easily exploited by hackers. Besides the financial losses these schemes create for hospitals, physicians, and insurance companies, there are also ongoing problems for patients whose records have been compromised. "When stolen identity information is used to seek medical care, diagnosis and treatment information is placed in the medical record," says Ashley Booth of Health Security Solutions. "These inaccuracies can affect future treatment decisions and diagnoses for the legitimate patient. Unlike credit cards which can be cancelled, allowing identity theft victims to begin afresh, medical records are continuous, ever-changing archives of information."[21]

"Unlike credit cards which can be cancelled, allowing identity theft victims to begin afresh, medical records are continuous, ever-changing archives of information."[21]

—Ashley Booth, representative for Health Security Solutions.

With medical records perpetually linked to numbers such as SSNs, driver's license numbers, or birth dates, the fraudulent procedures and medications that hackers obtain continue to appear in the files of the legitimate patient, often without the patient's knowledge. This can be particularly dangerous if, for example, a patient is in critical condition in an emergency room, and the doctor consults a record that is tainted by identity theft. The file might include bogus prior treatments or fail to indicate crucial drug allergies. And it is nearly impossible to clear up a medical record once medical identity theft has occurred. If a hacker's false information gets into a patient's file, it becomes difficult to separate bogus from legitimate data. "Medical identity theft has the potential to impede your medical treatment and the potential to kill you," says Robin Slade of the Medical Identity Fraud Alliance. "A thief using your identity may have a different blood type, or not have the same allergies. It's a fraud that causes your medical record to get contaminated by a perpetrator."[22] The difficulty patients have in reversing the damage caused by medical identity theft makes data security and theft prevention all the more urgent for health care officials. Experts say that stealing personal medical data can be so easy to accomplish and so difficult to uncover that tens of thousands of fake claims might be paid before authorities are aware of any crime. For this reason, they urge patients constantly to monitor their medical records and insurance statements for suspicious charges or other irregularities.

Other Hacking Schemes Related to Medical Records

Doctors and patients should be aware that hackers may also profit from accessing medical files by engaging in blackmail and extortion. In the United Kingdom sophisticated hackers steal medical records from the databases of the National Health Service (NHS) and search for the confidential files of rich and powerful individuals who have been diagnosed with diseases such as HIV that might carry a social stigma if publicly revealed. The hackers then send blackmail notes to the victims—usually businesspeople, politicians, or celebrities—threatening to go public with the information unless a ransom is paid.

Hacking Implanted Medical Devices

Some of the most unusual health care–related targets for hackers are implanted medical devices (IMDs), such as pacemakers, defibrillators, and insulin pumps. These devices can be programmed wirelessly so that they can be monitored from a distance. If they need to be adjusted or replaced, this is done in a doctor's office or clinic, where access is secure due to cryptographic (coding) techniques. There are concerns, however, that hackers could break the codes and gain wireless access to such devices for all sorts of malicious reasons. Some experts fear that hackers could threaten to tamper with IMDs as part of a blackmail scheme or could simply vandalize the devices with random attacks. Protecting the devices with more sophisticated coding would use up more of their processing power, thus running down batteries and requiring more frequent replacements.

As modern life becomes increasingly computerized, IMDs that perform a range of services doubtless will grow more common. Implants may soon be used in healthy people to detect problems before they become life threatening. Researchers are working on various methods to improve security for such devices. One possible solution is a microcontroller that derives a random password from the patient's heartbeat that can only be computed when touching the patient. "We have shown that the heartbeat has enough randomness to be used as a random number generator," says Professor Farinaz Koushanfar of Rice University. Thus a patient's own heartbeat could be used to foil the schemes of malicious hackers.

Quoted in R. Colin Johnson, "Foiling Medical Implant Hackers," *EE Times,* September 24, 2013. www.eetimes.com.

Such cases almost never make the news because of privacy concerns. The NHS has repeatedly affirmed its commitment to keeping patient files secure. Yet a new system in which NHS data is shared with research groups and private companies has led to worries that sensitive medical records are more vulnerable than ever.

Information about cosmetic surgery is another attractive blackmail target for hackers. In March 2014 hackers broke into servers belonging to the Harley Medical Group, which has a chain of cosmetic surgery clinics in the United Kingdom. Hacking into the company's website inquiry form, the cyberthieves accessed data for nearly a half-million patients, including names, addresses, dates of birth, e-mail addresses and phone numbers, and details of procedures that were being contemplated. Patients interested in getting cosmetic surgery fill in a form online before an appointment. After accessing the data, the hackers then tried—unsuccessfully—to extort payment from the company to keep the hackers from going public with embarrassing information about Harley's clients. Security experts say the company's clients are also ripe for blackmail, since they are generally wealthy and probably keen to avoid publicity about any inquiries they have made about cosmetic surgery. "Such information could be used not just to embarrass an individual, but also—potentially—to extort money from them," says veteran security expert Graham Cluley. "Furthermore, the private information could be sold to tabloid newspapers or entertainment websites which are scrabbling for some showbiz tittle tattle to fill their pages."[23]

Hackers also can insert a virus into medical files that makes them unreadable. For example, The Surgeons of Lake County, a small medical practice in an affluent northern Illinois suburb, suffered an attack by hackers who broke into its network, encrypted medical records, and then posted a message to the firm demanding a ransom payment in exchange for the password. This type of attack saves hackers the trouble of actually stealing and reselling the data. Instead they simply wall it off from its owners. Although authorities recommend calling law enforcement for help in such cases, hospitals and doctors' offices have such an urgent need to access patients' files that they are more likely to pay the ransom at once. Attacks like the one on The Surgeons of Lake County have led some to question the wisdom of digitizing medical files, fearing that malicious hackers could destroy patient records. Nevertheless, experts insist that while such incidents are worrisome the overall benefits of moving to electronic medical records far outweigh the problems.

New Concerns About Electronic Medical Records

A key aspect of health care reform in the United States has been the emphasis on making health records digital and available to be shared by providers. Almost three hundred state and regional health information exchanges (HIEs) provide doctors and other health care professionals with rapid access to data. An important goal of the Patient Protection and Affordable Care Act, which President Barack Obama signed into law in 2010, is to hasten and streamline the use of electronic protected health information. Yet some experts fear that new problems with ePHI security may result from the troubled rollout of the Affordable Care Act. Malfunctions and design flaws in the online insurance marketplaces, both federal and state, may have allowed hackers and other unauthorized individuals to access applicants' private medical information.

In January 2014 David Kennedy, head of a large computer security firm, testified before Congress about the security problems related to the Affordable Care Act. Kennedy declared that the HealthCare.gov website that enrollees use to apply for health insurance was completely vulnerable to hackers. He claimed that he was able to access

A senior applies for health insurance on the HealthCare.gov website. The site was found to be vulnerable to hacking.

seventy thousand personal records on the government website within about four minutes using a standard web browser and could have chosen to view thousands more. According to Kennedy, the website contained more than twenty security flaws that hackers could exploit. Hackers could steal personal information, illegally modify data, or attack the personal computers of those who used the website. Kennedy's testimony came two months after he and other expert witnesses advised the government to shut down the site in order to fix the problems. Kevin Mitnick, once the world's most wanted hacker and now a consultant on cybersecurity issues, agreed with Kennedy's concerns. "HealthCare.gov retrieves information from numerous third-party databases belonging to the IRS, Social Security Administration, Department of Homeland Security, and other State agencies," Mitnick observed in written testimony to Congress. "A breach may result in massive identity theft never seen before—these databases house information on every U.S. citizen!"[24] In February 2014 e-mails and other documents obtained by reporters showed that more than two-thirds of the state data systems that were supposed to tap into federal computers to verify applicants' personal information for coverage were rated as a high risk for security problems by government experts. By March 2014 the Department of Health and Human Services, the agency responsible for the HealthCare.gov website, insisted that the problems had been addressed and that the site is monitored by tools that will prevent any unauthorized access. Yet the agency refused to answer specific questions about security measures, and many experts remain skeptical that sensitive personal information is being properly protected.

> "HealthCare.gov retrieves information from numerous third-party databases belonging to the IRS, Social Security Administration, Department of Homeland Security, and other State agencies. A breach may result in massive identity theft never seen before—these databases house information on every U.S. citizen!"[24]
>
> *—Kevin Mitnick, former criminal hacker and now consultant on cybersecurity.*

Another concern with HIEs is that an exchange might sell patients' private data for profit. Privacy advocates warn that confidential medical records are coveted by many groups, including pharmaceutical companies, insurers, and medical researchers. Health exchanges with unstable finances might view data sales as a good source of revenue. Recently the United Kingdom's National Health Service announced a program called Care.data that will make patient data available for sale to drug companies and insurance firms. Experts worry that such schemes could lead the public to wonder who has their medical data and how it is being used. Patients might lie to their doctors or withhold information for fear of it falling into the wrong hands. Sales of personal medical records could also result in increased opportunities for identity theft.

The growing problem of medical identity theft shows how hackers are constantly seeking data sources that are vulnerable and potentially lucrative. It is the job of data security experts to stay one step ahead of the hackers by shoring up cyberdefenses and keeping information safe from prying eyes.

Chapter 5

Protections Against Hacking

People who read newspapers or watch network news programs might be forgiven for worrying that their personal data is more insecure than ever. Each day seems to bring new revelations about hacking schemes and data breaches on a grand scale. One such story that attracted worldwide attention early in 2014 was the discovery of a potentially devastating computer bug nicknamed Heartbleed. The bug (which is a software flaw, not a virus) creates a vulnerability in a widely used piece of software called OpenSSL, which is employed for security on many popular web servers. OpenSSL allows websites to transfer a visitor's sensitive information, including user name and password, back and forth from the website to the visitor's own computer in encrypted form so that outsiders cannot read it. The Heartbleed bug was introduced—apparently innocently—by one of the software's original programmers. It enables individuals such as malicious hackers to retrieve data from a server's memory without leaving a trace. Originally the bug was believed to have affected more than 60 percent of all Internet servers, but experts now have reduced that estimate to less than 18 percent—which still represents an enormous number of servers. Once the bug was discovered, the software was quickly patched, meaning it is no longer vulnerable. Still, the stories left people in a quandary about the security of their data. "Now, the important question is: Should you worry about this problem?" writes Jose Andrade, a founding editor on the technology site Engadget. "The short answer is: 'Yes, but don't panic.' You should definitely change your passwords at least for the services confirmed as vulnerable. . . . But you should be changing your passwords regularly no matter what."[25] As Andrade notes, some of the most effective protections against hacking are simply practical precautions that the average computer user should take.

Keeping Passwords Secure

One precaution that helps to foil hackers is keeping passwords and other log-in information protected from outsiders. As cybersecurity expert Joshua Cannell writes, "When it comes to your digital life, passwords hold the keys. While new technology emerges, like biometric scanners and smart cards, the password is still the most commonly used form of authentication since it is both cheap and easy to implement."[26] Managing passwords properly is vital to cybersecurity. A person should never have the password or PIN associated with a card written on the card itself. Keeping passwords on sticky notes next to a computer at home or in the office should also be avoided. Another simple rule for individuals is to not use the same password on different services. Users often worry about forgetting passwords

The Heartbleed bug information website is displayed on a cell phone and a laptop. The bug turned out to be a software flaw created by one of the software's original programmers.

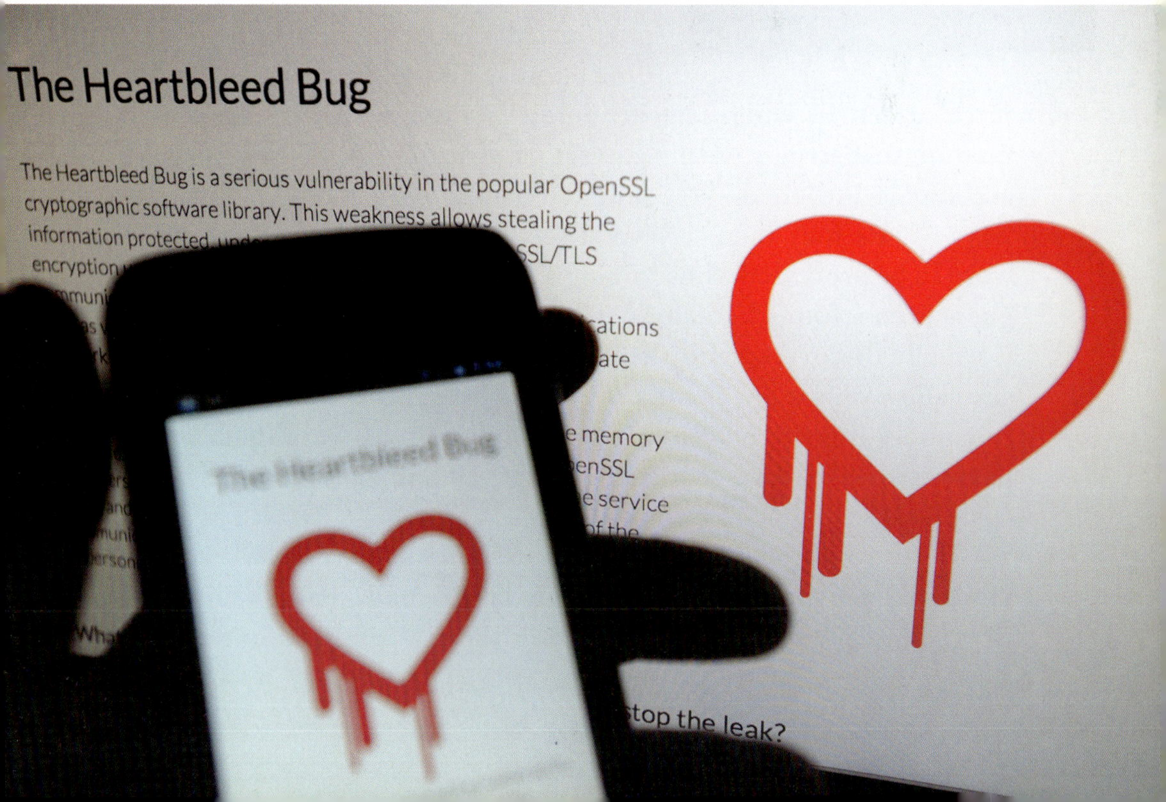

or managing an array of them. Today, however, there are applications that help people manage their passwords. An app called 1Password keeps passwords for banks, credit card companies, and other websites safely locked away. It protects bank account numbers, e-mail data, and passwords for wireless routers. It also includes a secure browser that will enter correct passwords automatically on financial sites such as online banks and brokerages. For users who fear their passwords are too simple, the app can even generate more complex passwords using combinations of upper and lowercase letters and random numbers. (Some apps's sole function is to produce long, tricky passwords using high-powered calculations.) And of course the 1Password app itself is protected by a password in case the user's smart phone were to fall into the wrong hands.

"Now, the important question is: Should you worry about this problem? The short answer is: 'Yes, but don't panic.' You should definitely change your passwords at least for the services confirmed as vulnerable. . . . But you should be changing your passwords regularly no matter what."[25]

—Jose Andrade, a founding editor for the technology site Engadget.

Taking precautions about passwords is necessary because hackers have sophisticated means to ferret them out. One popular ploy is the so-called "brute force" attack, in which a hacker employs software that tries repeated random text strings until a correct password is found and a private account is breached. Websites fend off such attacks in different ways. A site may require several seconds for each guess at a password to be processed, thus forcing a hacker to spend hours trying to guess even a four-character password. In the meantime, the attack is usually discovered and the account is shut down. Well-designed sites allow only a few incorrect guesses before they require the user to contact the site by e-mail. Some sites use software that creates passwords based on a sequence of encrypted images to quash brute force attacks.

The most sophisticated defenses are useless, however, when individuals fall prey to phishing scams and fake e-mails that ask for sensitive passwords. A person should never input a password in response

Dealing with Identity Theft

Anyone can be victimized by identity theft. In such a case, an individual should act promptly to repair the damage. The victim's first step is to ask one of the three credit reporting companies to place a fraud alert on his or her credit report. The company that is contacted is required to notify the other two credit reporting companies. This notification makes it difficult for an identity thief to open other fraudulent accounts in the victim's name. With an alert on a person's report, a business must verify the person's identity before issuing new credit. The initial alert remains on a person's report for at least ninety days. Next, the victim should order a free credit report from each of the credit reporting companies. Each company should be asked to include only the last four digits of the victim's Social Security number. The credit reports likely will show unauthorized charges or accounts. Finally, the victim should create an Identity Theft Report. This report helps the victim deal with credit reporting companies, debt collectors, and businesses and websites that have provided the identity thief with credit. The Identity Theft Report can also help the victim remove fraudulent information from his or her credit report and stop a company from collecting bogus debts resulting from the incident. Instructions on how to create an Identity Theft Report are found on the Federal Trade Commission (FTC) website.

to an e-mail request or a pop-up screen. Any suspicious requests for a password or other personal data should be reported to the appropriate business or website immediately.

More-Secure Credit Card Transactions

Consumers are also seeking better protection for their credit card information after the recent hacking of credit card data at Target and Neiman Marcus stores. Those massive data breaches showed how vulnerable magnetic stripe cards are to hacking schemes. It so happens that the United States is one of the only countries in the world still using mostly magnetic stripe cards. Almost every other nation has gone to EMV cards with so-called smart-card technology. EMV cards—named after Europay, MasterCard, and Visa, the original developers—are equipped with a microprocessor chip that encrypts personal information, such as account numbers, that is transferred to the merchant. The key is that the data is encoded differently each time the card is used. According to Credit Card Forum, a website that reviews credit card plans and security, "Even if thieves manage to get data from a merchant (as they did in the Target breach), it's like stealing an expired password—useless. EMV chips are also tougher to clone than magnetic stripes are."[27]

Until recently, neither merchants, card issuers, nor consumers in the United States showed much enthusiasm for switching to EMV smart cards. The technology has been around since the 1990s, but EMV cards are more expensive to produce and few stores have in-

A recent hacking of Target's payment card data showed the flaws in the magnetic strip credit card system. The United States is one of the few countries that continue to use the now outdated technology.

vested in payment terminals that accept them. Only Americans who travel overseas have been using them. That seems likely to change as more and more banks and credit card companies introduce EMV cards. The US version employs "chip and signature" technology, requiring a signature for each transaction, which differs from Europe's "chip and PIN" that calls for the card user to type in a number. Of course, EMV cards offer no special protection unless merchants update their payment terminals. To pressure them to do just that, the major card networks have announced that after October 2015 banks and merchants that have not upgraded to EMV will themselves be liable for any losses from data theft or credit fraud.

While EMV smart cards certainly make the job of a hacker or data thief more difficult, they do not offer foolproof safeguards. Evidence from Europe shows that credit card scammers still succeed by conducting transactions by Internet, mail order, or telephone that do not require a physical card. Even with EMV cards, consumers should carefully check their card statements each month for unauthorized purchases or withdrawals.

Anti-hacking Laws and Policies

While a person's own vigilance is a strong defense against hackers, law enforcement also plays a major role in preventing or uncovering hacking attacks. There are many federal and state laws governing hacking and illegal access to personal data. The computer revolution and the rise of the Internet have led legislators to update old statutes to address cybercrime or create new laws that specifically deal with the latest technology. The first federal law to address cybercrime specifically is the Computer Fraud and Abuse Act (CFAA), which was passed in 1986 at the beginning of the personal computer era. The CFAA makes it illegal to access a computer knowingly without authorization, to exceed authorized use of a computer system, to steal financial data via computer, or to commit fraud or extortion via computer. A 1994 change in the CFAA dealt with offenders who sought to transmit code that causes damage to a computer system—i.e., viruses, worms, and other malware. Overall the CFAA outlaws online trespassing by hackers who break in to computer systems to steal or vandalize data. Penalties for violators are severe, with prison sentences ranging from five years to life.

The CFAA drew national attention in January 2013 when an Internet activist and hacker named Aaron Swartz committed suicide after being indicted on charges related to hacking the network at the Massachusetts Institute of Technology. Swartz claimed he downloaded more than 2 million documents from MIT in order to make the scholarly material freely available online. Critics of the prosecution said that Swartz's threatened prison term of thirty-five years was too harsh for what was essentially an act of civil disobedience. They insisted that the CFAA's definitions of what constitutes unauthorized access were too loose. Supporters of the law, however, noted that Swartz had deliberately used false information to gain unauthorized access and commit theft. One problem with the CFAA is that different courts have reached opposite conclusions on whether the law can be used to target individuals who use valid access privileges to steal or misuse data from an employer or client. According to Eric Goldman, a professor at the Santa Clara University School of Law in California, "Anyone who misrepresents their name, age, location or other information when signing up for a web service is in a sense violating that site's terms of service and could theoretically at least be in violation of the CFAA. We have this very broad federal anti-trespassing statute that is incredibly powerful."[28] Goldman thinks the CFAA empowers officials to prosecute comparatively minor offenses.

"Anyone who misrepresents their name, age, location or other information when signing up for a web service is in a sense violating that site's terms of service and could theoretically at least be in violation of the CFAA. We have this very broad federal anti-trespassing statute that is incredibly powerful."[28]

—Eric Goldman, law professor at Santa Clara University.

Several other laws deal with information privacy in today's world of computer networks and wireless communications. The Electronic Communications Privacy Act (ECPA), also passed in 1986, expands the Federal Wiretap Act to address the growing use of computer sys-

Hacker Aaron Swartz committed suicide after being sentenced to thirty-five years in prison for his involvement in hacking the computer network of the Massachusetts Institute of Technology.

tems to communicate and transfer data, including innovations such as cell phone calls, voice mail, e-mail, and other wireless technologies. The ECPA also protects stored information, such as e-mail messages on a server. One clause in the ECPA allows an Internet service provider (ISP) to intercept messages when it suspects they are being used to spread a virus or otherwise damage its system. The Cyber Security Enhancement Act (CSEA), passed in 2002 together with the Homeland Security Act, gives law enforcement extensive powers to deal with cybercrime and increases penalties for violations under the CFAA. Before passage of the CSEA, ISPs could not reveal the contents of e-mails or personal details about customers stored on their servers without a search warrant from the government. The CSEA

Foiling Hackers with Quantum Encryption

Certain researchers think quantum encryption may be the ultimate safeguard against hackers. The idea is to use a system of communicating between parties on the Internet based on laws of physics. Ordinary encryption methods rely on scrambling a message in such a way that it can only be unscrambled by way of a secret key. Hackers set themselves the task of figuring out these secret keys. And while modern non-quantum encryption methods can be fiendishly complex, they do have weaknesses that math-savvy hackers can exploit. With continual advances in computing power and new decoding software, hackers have a fighting chance to unlock any standard method of encryption. Quantum encryption offers a solution to these weak spots. The key is coded into a series of particles called photons that are passed between two sharers trying to communicate secretly. A basic principle of quantum physics ensures that a hacker or unauthorized user cannot view these photons without altering or destroying them. In theory, quantum encryption is foolproof. "In this case, it doesn't matter what technology the adversary has, they'll never be able to break the laws of physics," says Richard Hughes, a physicist at Los Alamos National Laboratory in New Mexico.

However, quantum encryption turns out to have its own problems. For example, a hacker can basically blind a photon detector with a strong pulse, rendering it incapable of reading the photon-based code. Nevertheless, scientists remain hopeful that quantum technology is the key to hacker-proof encryption.

Quoted in *Wired*, "Laws of Physics Say Quantum Cryptography Is Unhackable. It's Not," June 7, 2013. www.wired.com.

enables law enforcement officials and government agents to access data without a warrant if an ISP has reason to believe the information is connected to a serious crime. The CSEA also lets an ISP authorize law enforcement officials to intercept electronic data on its servers if the ISP suspects the data belongs to an unauthorized hacker. The Economic Espionage Act (EEA), passed in 1996, focuses on those who knowingly commit an offense that benefits a foreign government or who misappropriate trade secrets or data. While not targeting computer crime and hackers specifically, the EEA covers the use of computers to steal sensitive information.

Among laws that deal with data theft are federal statutes covering the safety and privacy of medical information. As mentioned previously, the Health Insurance Portability and Accountability Act (HIPAA) and the Health Information Technology for Economic and Clinical Health Act (HITECH) both address the security and confidentiality of health care records.

In addition to these laws related to hacking, the US Justice Department is seeking greater authority to hack into computers on its own during criminal investigations. Justice Department officials want rules to allow federal agents greater leeway to access the computers of suspected felons not individually but in groups. The rule changes would address cases in which anonymous hackers use botnets—groups of hijacked computers—forcing investigators to search many computers at once using a single warrant. The new approach would include the ability to insert malware onto suspects' computers. While supporters claim this change would merely bring laws regarding legal searches into the computer age, civil liberties advocates fear that the privacy of innocent individuals would be endangered under such a proposal. "I don't think many Americans would be comfortable with the government sending code onto their computers without their knowledge or consent,"[29] says Nathan Freed Wessler, a lawyer for the American Civil Liberties Union. Some fear that overzealous efforts to protect people from hackers can be just as dangerous as a criminal invasion of privacy.

> "I don't think many Americans would be comfortable with the government sending code onto their computers without their knowledge or consent."[29]
>
> *—Nathan Freed Wessler, lawyer for the American Civil Liberties Union.*

Basic Safeguards Against Hackers

While law enforcement officials resort to more drastic measures to combat hackers, individuals can help safeguard their personal information by taking simple precautions. Here are some suggestions for protecting online accounts against hackers:

- Use an Internet connection that is secure. Almost all Internet service providers use a communications protocol called Hypertext Transfer Protocol Secure (HTTPS), which automatically encrypts each Internet connection. For increased security, an individual can use a virtual private network (VPN) to encrypt data and guarantee anonymity. Every user should be aware that hackers use rogue Wi-Fi access points to access all of a computer's traffic. Bogus log-in screens can prompt users to type in their passwords. Each user should also ensure that his or her home Wi-Fi setup is up to date and protected with an effective password. Old routers should be replaced with more advanced models to foil hackers.
- Keep computers and networks free from malware. Viruses of various kinds are used to gather log-ins and passwords and deliver them to hackers. Users should install antivirus and browser protection software to safeguard their computers.
- Use passwords wisely. Hackers are expert at exploiting foolish or lazy practices regarding authentication. Users should choose strong passwords that employ combinations of upper and lowercase letters and numbers, should use different passwords for different sites, should change passwords regularly, and should take care in how they store and share passwords. As mentioned, apps for managing passwords across several online sites or services can be a useful protection from hackers.
- Set up and maintain a strong primary e-mail account. Users should make careful notes on the information provided to register an account. If possible, a user should write and answer his or her own security question so that hackers cannot find the answer by searching through personal information online. Financial documents, passwords, and other important data should never be stored in e-mails. Individuals should be alert to spam e-mails that hackers send to their contacts using their e-mail addresses. They should never click on suspicious links or attachments in e-mails that might be phishing scams.

- Engage in prompt damage control. If a user suspects a hacking attack has occurred, she or he should immediately change all passwords and security questions from a computer or other device that is known to be free from malware. Using an infected computer will simply allow hackers to capture the new passwords and information. Users should not refrain from telling others about a hacking attack. There is no shame in suffering such an attack, and sharing information about what happened can help prevent future attacks.

The Future of Privacy and Hacking

As computer links for every conceivable function continue to expand, ingenious hackers keep finding new ways of attacking people's privacy. One ripe field is the automobile computer, which is employed for everything from navigation assistance to speed control.

Two professional hackers bored with pointing out bugs in software have turned to isolating potential problems with computer systems in automobiles. Charlie Miller and Chris Valasek prepared a report on computer flaws in the Toyota Prius and Ford Escape. By hacking into the Prius's computer system, the pair were able to jerk the car's steering wheel, make it accelerate suddenly, or force it to brake while traveling at 80 miles an hour (129 kph). They also managed to disable the Escape's brakes entirely when it was traveling at slow speeds. The potential for hackers to disrupt onboard systems makes the idea of self-driving, computer-run cars much less appealing.

The ease and convenience of the computerized world has to be balanced against the ever-present dangers of hacking, data sabotage, and identity theft. Every advance in encryption and data security seems to be countered by some insidious new malware or hacking scheme. The website a user logs in to may be attacked by a hacker located halfway around the world. The best way to maintain online privacy is to keep passwords and log-in information protected and constantly be alert to suspicious schemes. Personal information may never be completely safe from hackers, but prudent measures by government officials, private companies, and individuals can make hacking more difficult and less profitable overall.

Source Notes

Introduction: A Holiday Hacking Attack

1. Michael Riley, Ben Elgin, Dune Lawrence, and Carol Matlack, "Missed Alarms and 40 Million Stolen Credit Card Numbers: How Target Blew It," *Bloomberg Businessweek*, March 13, 2014. www.businessweek.com.
2. Quoted in Riley, Elgin, Lawrence, and Matlack, "Missed Alarms and 40 Million Stolen Credit Card Numbers."
3. Quoted in Sharon Jayson, "Online and Mobile Dating Face Privacy, Safety Concerns," *USA Today*, March 27, 2014. www.usatoday.com.

Chapter 1: A Look at Privacy Concerns

4. Quoted in NDTV Gadgets, "US Internet Users More Worried About Hacking than Privacy: Survey," December 20, 2013. http://gadgets.ndtv.com.
5. Frederick S. Lane, *American Privacy: The 400-Year History of Our Most Contested Right*. Boston: Beacon, 2009, p. 80.
6. Federal Judicial Center: History of the Federal Judiciary, "Dissenting Opinion of Justice Louis D. Brandeis in *Olmstead v. United States*." www.fjc.gov.
7. Robert Siciliano, "Social Security Number: All-Purpose Identifier," Robert Siciliano website, November 28, 2011. http://robertsiciliano.com.
8. Susan Krauss Whitbourne, "The High Cost of Facebook Exhibitionism," *Psychology Today*, April 9, 2013. www.psychologytoday.com.

Chapter 2: How Hackers Operate

9. Quoted in Zach Miners, "EA Games Site Hacked to Steal Apple IDs," *PCWorld*, March 19, 2014. www.pcworld.com.

10. Quoted in Alejandro Martinez-Cabrera, "Cyber-Criminals Don't Need Technical Skills," *SFGate*, March 14, 2010. www.sfgate.com.
11. Quoted in J. Craig Anderson, "Identity Theft Growing, Costly to Victims," *USA Today*, April 14, 2013. www.usatoday.com.
12. Roger A. Grimes, "7 Sneak Attacks Used by Today's Most Devious Hackers," InfoWorld, September 30, 2013. www.infoworld.com.
13. Quoted in Josh Halliday, "Game Over for Anonymous Hackers Who Thought They Would Never Be Caught," *Guardian*, January 25, 2013. www.theguardian.com.

Chapter 3: Hacking and Identity Theft

14. Lane, *American Privacy*, p. 243.
15. Adam Levin, "4 Big Problems with Social Security Numbers," *Huffington Post*, May 3, 2013. www.huffingtonpost.com.
16. Quoted in Tom Barlow, "Crooks Can Guess Digits in Your Social Security Number, Study Finds," *Daily Finance*, January 11, 2011. www.dailyfinance.com.
17. Quoted in Jaikumar Vijayan, "Target Hackers Try New Ways to Use Stolen Card Data," *Computerworld*, December 23, 2013. www.computerworld.com.
18. Quoted in Kelly Santos, "Fraud Files: Thieves Take Out Student Loans on Your Dime," *Identity Theft 911 Blog*, February 12, 2013. www.idt911blog.com.

Chapter 4: Hacking Personal Health Information

19. Quoted in Erin McCann, "Hackers Target Health Data in New Breach," *Healthcare IT News*, January 20, 2014. www.healthcareitnews.com.
20. Quoted in David Schultz, "As Patients Go Digital, Theft and Hacking Problems Grow," *Kaiser Health News*, June 3, 2012. www.kaiserhealthnews.org.
21. Ashley Booth, "An Increase in Targeted Hacking?," *Health Security Solutions*, September 3, 2013. www.healthsecuritysolutions.com.

22. Quoted in Jim Landers, "Medical Identity Theft Is Fast-Growing and Dangerous," *Dallas Morning News*, September 16, 2013. www.dallasnews.com.
23. Quoted in John Leyden, "Hackers Attempt to Blackmail Plastic Surgeons," *Register*, April 16, 2014. www.theregister.co.uk.
24. Quoted in Patrick Howley, "'World's Most Wanted Hacker' SLAMS Obamacare Website Security," *Daily Caller*, January 17, 2014. http://dailycaller.com.

Chapter 5: Protections Against Hacking

25. Jose Andrade, "What Is Heartbleed, Anyway?," *Engadget*, April 12, 2014. www.engadget.com.
26. Joshua Cannell, "Too Tough to Crack?," *Malwarebytes Unpacked* (blog), April 22, 2013. http://blog.malwarebytes.org.
27. Credit Card Forum, "Chip and PIN Credit Cards in the USA for 2014?," *The Blog*, March 17, 2014. http://creditcardforum.com.
28. Quoted in Jaikumar Vijayan, "Swartz Suicide Shines Light on Federal Anti-hacking Law," *Computerworld*, January 15, 2013. www.computerworld.com.
29. Quoted in Chris Strohm, "Federal Agents Seek to Loosen Rules on Hacking Computers," *Bloomberg*, May 9, 2014. www.bloomberg.com.

Online Privacy Tips

Basic Security

- Use security software to block viruses and malware. Keep it up-to-date.
- Use passwords at least eight characters long. Add numerals and punctuation to make them harder to guess.
- Back up important data to a flash or USB drive or an online service.

E-mail and Messaging

- Do not click on web links or attachments in e-mail or text messages unless you are expecting them (strange messages from a friend may indicate that their account has been "hijacked").
- Beware of "scary" messages that claim to be from a bank or government agency. Contact the agency directly if you think there might be a problem.
- Do not put credit card numbers or other sensitive information in e-mail or text messages.

Web and Social Networks

- Learn about browser features that can enhance security and privacy.
- Find and use the privacy settings for Facebook, Twitter, and other social networks.
- Do not post personal details or other information that you would not want a stranger to know.

Banking and E-commerce

- Make payments only on secure web pages (indicated by https:// in the address and a padlock icon).

- Do not do banking or online purchases on a public Wi-Fi network.
- Monitor bank and credit card accounts regularly for signs of fraud.

Mobile Devices

- Protect your phone or tablet with a passcode.
- Install software that allows you to track or disable lost or stolen devices.
- Install apps from only trusted sources.
- Check settings to see what information apps may be obtaining from your device.

Finally . . .

- Think before you hit "Send." You cannot take your words back.
- Common sense and courtesy can go a long way.

Related Organizations and Websites

Center for Cybercrime Studies

John Jay College of Criminal Justice
City University of New York
website: http//johnjayresearch.org

The Center for Cybercrime Studies seeks to raise awareness of risks, vulnerabilities, and protection requirements related to new information technologies and evaluate the effectiveness of methods to fight cybercrime.

Center for Identity Management and Information Protection (CIMIP)

Utica College
1600 Burrstone Rd.
Utica, NY 13502
phone: (315) 792-3231
e-mail: drebovich@utica.edu
website: www.utica.edu

The CIMIP is dedicated to researching identity management, information sharing, and data protection.

Federal Trade Commission (FTC)

600 Pennsylvania Ave. NW
Washington, DC 20580
phone: (202) 326-2222
website: www.ftc.gov

The FTC is a federal agency that includes the Bureau of Consumer Protection. It seeks to prevent business practices that are anticompetitive, deceptive, or unfair to consumers.

Identity Theft Resource Center (ITRC)

9672 Via Excelencia
San Diego, CA 92126
phone: (888) 400-5530
e-mail: itrc@idtheftcenter.org
website: www.idtheftcenter.org

The ITRC serves as a national resource on consumer issues related to cybersecurity, data breaches, social media, online fraud and scams, and other issues.

National Cyber Security Alliance (NCSA)

website: www.staysafeonline.org

The NCSA is a nonprofit organization that seeks to educate and empower a digital society to use the Internet safely and securely at home, work, and school.

Ponemon Institute

2308 US 31 N.
Traverse City, MI 49686
phone: (800) 887-3118
website: www.ponemon.org

The Ponemon Institute conducts independent research on privacy, data protection, and information security policy.

PrivacyMatters.com

9500 W. Dodge Rd., Suite 100
Omaha, NE 68114
phone: (800) 436-0817
e-mail: membersavings@privacypatters.com
website: www.privacymatters.com

The PrivacyMatters.com website provides credit management advice and identity theft protection products and services.

SANS Institute

8120 Woodmont Ave., Suite 205
Bethesda, MD 20814
phone: (301) 654-7267
e-mail: info@sans.org
website: www.sans.org

A research and education organization, the SANS Institute is one of the largest sources for information security training and security certification in the world.

For Further Research

Books

Douglas Jacobson and Joseph Idziorek, *Computer Security Literacy: Staying Safe in a Digital World*. Boca Raton, FL: CRC, 2013.

Frederick S. Lane, *American Privacy: The 400-Year History of Our Most Contested Right*. Boston: Beacon, 2009.

Theresa M. Payton and Theodore Claypool, *Privacy in the Age of Big Data*. Lanham, MD: Rowman & Littlefield, 2014.

Kevin Poulsen, *Kingpin: How One Hacker Took Over the Billion-Dollar Cybercrime Underground*. New York: Crown, 2011.

Georgia Weidman, *Penetration Testing: A Hands-On Introduction to Hacking*. San Francisco: No Starch, 2014.

Steve Weisman, *50 Ways to Protect Your Identity in a Digital Age: New Financial Threats You Need to Know and How to Avoid Them*. Upper Saddle River, NJ: FT, 2013.

Websites

Computerworld (www.computerworldcom). A variety of topics related to computers and the Internet, including the latest news on cybercrime and hacking, are covered on this site.

Engadget (www.engadget.com). This site includes articles about every aspect of computer technology, including malware and protection against data theft.

Identity Theft Action Plan (www.identitytheftactionplan.com). Created by the Pennsylvania Commission on Crime and Delinquency, this site provides helpful tips and resources about how to prevent identity theft and how to respond if identity theft occurs.

Kaiser Health News (www.kaiserhealthnews.org). This site features articles about current issues involving medical identity theft and how to protect medical records from hackers.

Mashable (http://mashable.com). Articles about every aspect of online privacy and social media are available on this site.

PC (www.pcmag.com). This online magazine includes the latest news about personal computers and online security.

Prevent and Report Identity Theft (www.usa.gov). Information on how to report identity theft and how seniors can avoid becoming victims of identity theft is provided on this US government site.

World Privacy Forum (www.worldprivacyforum). This site covers a wide range of topics related to privacy and hacking, including medical identity theft and data privacy for individuals.

Index

Note: Boldface page numbers indicate illustrations.